In Two Minds?

How Tarot can help
you decide

Thorvi Damle

BEEJA
HOUSE

BEEJA
H O U S E

Copyright © **Thorvi Damle 2022**

ISBN: **978-93-93635-25-9**

Any references to historical events, real people, or real places are used fictitiously. Names, characters and places are the product of the author's imagination.

Published by: Beeja House

First Printing Edition 2022

Author Email: thorvimdamle@gmail.com

www.thorvidamle.com

Table of Contents

Dedication

This book is dedicated to all who strive to improve in life, who do not rely on luck alone and are willing to take action to change their circumstances. Are you someone who waits for the tide to turn or builds a boat that rides?

Questions to ponder on

- Do you feel stuck in life? In terms of career, finances, relationships, like you know you can improve but do not seem to find the exact way?
- Do you feel undervalued at work or home? You put in a lot of effort but you are not appreciated?
- Do you battle your actions versus intentions in your mind? Is this right or wrong?
- Do you need someone to validate your gut feeling? You know that it is the correct option but need that extra push to go for it?
- Are you going through a divorce or a separation that is causing a lot of overwhelming emotions?
- Are you afraid to commit and yet unable to let go of your love interest?
- Are you at a crossroads in your career? With many options and yet no conclusive option?
- Wondering whether to enter into a business partnership with someone, how will it span out?
- Have you started losing hope in a relationship or struggling with a family member?
- Wondering how compatible you are before you marry the person?

Do any of these questions resonate? Has any decision caused you stress and sleepless nights? If your answer is "yes", then this book is for you.

Thorvi Damle, who has helped countless individuals cross the rocky bridges in life, brings a simple, uncomplicated approach to Tarot as a tool for analytics and diagnosis of life's challenges. The exciting part is, YOU will solve your problems. That too without the stress & drama, as she holds the mirror to your inner guidance system.

Ready to be empowered?

Introduction

"Everything you ever needed, need or will need can be found within you; you just need to look at the right plac." – Thorvi Damle

Oftentimes in life, we find ourselves struggling alone. We may have a big family or many friends and yet when it comes to critical life decisions or circumstances that have a huge impact on our lives, we find there is no simple answer to it. As a tarot practitioner, I work with many individuals helping them find their solutions. I started off like any other person, fascinated by the fortune-telling and predictive side of tarot, but slowly I realised the real power of this tool was beyond fortune-telling, it was in *deliberate living*. Creating a life that you want to live, with the circumstances given to you, it's like each of us was born in our own version of a video game, and we need to make the most of what we have. It may be health, wealth, relationships, talent, opportunities and so on. The potential for success is present in all of us, yet so many of us struggle through life.

As I changed my approach and became a trusted friend to my clients, I watched them bloom into the best versions of themselves. With each tarot session, I observed the increase in self-confidence, the questions changed from *"Why me?"* to *"What can I do to fix it?"* The complaining and blaming shifted to problem-solving and that made it extremely gratifying.

Mindsets do not change overnight and unfortunately, we cannot talk to our powerful subconscious mind to listen to us and change our thought patterns overnight, this is where the tarot plays a critical role. Clients I have worked with have not only solved the problems they were facing when they came to me, but they also elevated their lives and gained tremendous confidence that has in turn attracted more positive opportunities in life. The cycle need not always be vicious, a positive momentum can gain speed and create miracles.

This book is aimed at showcasing the power of tarot in changing your life. It is not intended to teach you tarot, you do not need to learn tarot to experience it. The book will walk you through the foundation of how you approach life, how you make the choices and decisions, what is causing the blockages and struggles, how you can improve the quality of your life and life decisions by simple changes, incorporating tarot into your decision-making process. We will discuss holistic decision making, decision fatigue, the four steps to elevate method that you can start applying instantly to your life. On the tarot front, we will bust myths, answer questions on what is tarot, what to expect in a tarot session, psychology of tarot etc. Enough information to help you find a good tarot practitioner and plan your next step in life.

I draw from my experiences, working in the corporate world for over 13 years, managing multicounty projects and having worked with people across the globe. I combine these learnings with experiences from a lifetime of spiritual, religious, intuitive and psychological studies and intense practices to approach tarot from both mind and psychic levels. We will be successful only when we approach a problem on all levels, not just the thinking plane.

A lot of people are missing out on opportunities and are struggling emotionally, mentally and even physically, all of which can be resolved by involving tarot as a friend, philosopher and guide. Free will is always present and you can choose to ignore or brush off tarot because in itself tarot will not solve your problems for you. You will need to take the action and make the choices, but without

GPS you cannot confidently explore unknown places of the world, let tarot be your GPS.

Are you ready to gain the knowledge that can open doors for you? Are you ready to step out of your misery and actually live life? Let's begin.

"Tarot is a way of sorting out what's bothering you and getting advice from the best-informed source - you - in a way that you're likely to listen to."

-Rosemary Edghill,
(Author of Speak Daggers to Her)

1

What Is Stopping You From That Spectacular Life?

"It is in your moments of decision that, your destiny is shaped"
-Tony Robbins

It is July 2020. In a suburban home in Bangalore, Gita is hurrying up to log in to her laptop for the day's work. She got up late as she was up late the night before handling a critical issue at work. She opens her Outlook and is hit by 100 unread emails. She can see the names and the subject lines and instantly knows how it is not going to be a cheerful day.

She is a developer working for a prestigious IT firm and has worked her way up in the organization. As she gulps down her coffee, she is skimming through the emails. There are some from the US stakeholders asking for an update, some from her manager asking her to create presentations for management meetings, some from the HR for a fun time which is ironic given her bandwidth, some from the finance department to file the IT returns, some from team members and junior resources with questions and a handful of emails, she has no clue why she was included in. She closes her eyes for a few seconds, takes a deep breath and reminds herself of the EMIs due, the bills to pay, why she needs this job, and starts the slow and tedious task of email reading and responding. It will take her a good hour before she can even start her work and even then she has a ton of meetings scheduled most of which add no value to her work. Sounds familiar? Pretty much the start of most days in a corporate professional's life.

The day began for Gita even before she logged in. She got up, did her basic chores of the morning and worked out at home as pretty much the entire world was in lockdown. Her mother had a list of groceries for her to order online along with medicines for her parents. The cylinder too had to be ordered soon, since the cooking gas was over. She called the gas agency several times and shared the location. Her mother was not happy that the cooking was stalled but on an alternative Gita had set up the induction stove for her mother along with a set of instructions on how to use it.

Gita is single, also a single child to her parents, who stay with her now. They moved to Bangalore from their hometown and found the big city a bit alien. They are out of their comfort zone and don't really know any neighbours or have any friends. The lockdown has not helped either, being senior citizens, they avoid going out. This means they are dependent on Gita for almost everything.

The breakfast is somehow cooked on the induction stove and it is time to log in. Gita just got off a call with her junior who drained her of all her mental energy by asking her the same questions. She had spent 3 months training him, it was like he had some short-term memory loss. Then she received a call from the cylinder delivery boy who was lost, despite having the precise GPS location. She spent the next 15 minutes guiding him to her house. She sometimes wondered if she would excel in the field of navigation, thanks to Bangalore roads and calls like these that started with "yel idhira sir?" (Where are you?). In another few minutes, the same drama was repeated for the grocery guy and the medical store delivery guy.

Meanwhile, her laptop kept pinging messages from team members on the chat with a series of questions on the project. She also had another meeting to attend within the next 5 minutes and had to prepare for it. She is trying hard to keep it together, when around 11.30 AM her mother walks in and asks her, *"What should we cook for lunch?"* and as if someone hit the big red button that shoots off the nuclear missile, the anger switch inside Gita flips on. She cannot take it anymore, she starts yelling at her mother, why can't her mother understand, why can't she decide this simple thing on her own, why did she need her all the time and it went on and on, her mother is shocked, she does not know why Gita is reacting like this to a simple question, she just leaves the room quietly.

Gita sits there fuming for a few minutes, then walks up to the other side of the room for a glass of water and immediately a wave of guilt hits her, why did she react so much for a simple question? What was happening? She had not intended to hurt her mother but she had done just that. The next few hours are spent in guilt and by the end of the day, she is tired, burnt out and miserable. She has a sudden craving for biryani and ice cream and ends up ordering in that evening a little extra portion than normal. Only after dinner and the last scoop of ice cream does she feel alive again, and somehow manages to log out before 10 PM that day.

The next day her friend calls her about an opportunity in another company, a more challenging role with better pay and though the interview process will be intensive, she is 100% sure Gita is the right candidate and will fit in well. She has heard Gita complain about her job way too many times and she feels strongly that Gita will do well in a new environment. Gita's response is that of fear and excitement but mostly fear, doubts clouding her mind, is she really prepared to take on a bigger role, can she handle a bigger challenge? Money is definitely nice to have, but she is comfortable in her present role, miserable but comfortable. Basically, she is used to being comfortably miserable. This opportunity instead of bringing hope and excitement brings on more stress, confusion and fear. She battles it internally for two days and then starts discussing it with friends and family. They give her their opinions based on their experiences and she gets mixed reviews that confuses her even more. A tiny voice within her has been asking her to move and take up new opportunities, but her brain overpowers it and external factors and stressors tape it shut.

Finally, after a week, she tells her friend that she is comfortable at her current job, at least she has a salary coming in every month. This is a known devil and she wants to just continue till the next appraisal cycle, anyways she is not qualified enough, she will never be selected and so on. All Gita wants to do is run away, win the lottery and go live on an island, at least, plan a beach getaway to just drink, eat and sleep. A vacation that will solve all the issues in life.

Does the story resonate a bit? What do you think happened here? Why did a smart capable young professional choose to step away from a growth opportunity? How will this decision impact the rest of her life? Why did she react like that towards her mother's question? Regardless of gender, people all over the world are facing such days, experiencing stress on some level and reacting or misplacing anger on close relationships.

Lack of the right decision-making skills is stopping us from leading that spectacular life we all deserve.

Decision. A very serious word for the ears yet a daily part of life. Right from what to wear to whom to marry, the complexity and the frequency varies. One cannot avoid making decisions, making choices, taking action, it is all a part of being human. But what we do not realise is that every decision is small or big only for our intellect, for the brain it amounts to the same amount of effort and stress. Yes, you read it correctly, *our brains perceive every decision with the same intensity although it is not apparent.*

We use the term burn out, stressed, tired, demotivated, running the rat race and we usually talk of quick fixes or band-aids like a holiday, a few days of a staycation or going to the spa etc. and all of these, help only for a short while. We never really look at developing tools to empower people to become better decision-makers and avoid burnout in the first place.

Although it is a huge part of being a human, decision making is still elusive in nature, we do not know a lot about how humans make decisions. Decisions are not always backed by data or logic and are not always left-brained. There is a lot of research being conducted especially in the last 10 years on decision making and its effects on our lives and how we can get better at it. Decisions look very logical brain-based but there are times a person is unable to provide any explanation to the decisions he takes, he himself is unaware of why he took that step or did not take that step. Especially, time-bound decisions like a doctor working in an emergency room, even if there are protocols set up by the hospitals, to save a patient the doctor may need to go around these protocols, and his/her gut-feeling is what pushes the decisions.

How does a bad decision affect us?

A single decision looked at on its own can seem insignificant in the long run. Like with our friend Gita from earlier, if you look at her decision of not attending the interview as a lone incident, then it is no big deal, she will get other opportunities. But her decision will make her less likely to consider the next opportunity and then the next opportunity and her excuses will become self-actualized. She will keep postponing this till the next appraisal cycle every year and continue being miserable, affecting her quality of life and mental health in the long run. She will experience anxiety and stress every time she is presented with a new opportunity and she will face sleepless nights, stress-induced headaches and a whole lot of miserable symptoms. If only she had an ally who could show her the bigger picture, empower her with the right information, remove the cloud of confusion and avoid all the stress and drama around a situation? If someone had told her that she should destress, delegate tasks at work as well as at home and go for that interview, an assurance that things are not as bad as they seem, that she has the capacity to go ahead and if she does not do this, how this will affect her in the long term. All she needed was to understand her current situation, her strengths, the probability of success, focus area and underlying blocks in her thought process and environment, she would have succeeded. Like someone holding a magnifying glass and suddenly things that looked murky are now crystal clear.

Now imagine if you had such an ally, someone who can help you without judging you, someone who can validate your thoughts, someone who can point you in the right direction, help you avoid all the stress and drama, instead help you focus on what is more important. Wouldn't this be magical? Someone that can raise your chances of winning in life almost instantly? You need not imagine anymore, this book will introduce you to that ally in the form of Tarot and how it can elevate your life. Looking beyond fortune-telling, how tarot can dig deeper into our thoughts and get the right answers and directions for our life path, be it in career, relationship, health, finance, property, legal disputes, marriage, pets, any and all aspects of our lives. Tarot can be that analytical and diagnostic tool that can fill the gap and accelerate your growth.

But before we dive into tarot, let us understand what the gap is and how it is affecting our chances at a spectacular life.

Our life is not what happens to us, it is how we respond to what happens to us. This response or the choice we make has a profound effect on our destiny. In this sense, it is like a dotted drawing book for kids, an image is created by joining the dots. If each dot is a decision in your life, then the final image depends on the placement and quality of each dot and how you join each of these dots. Successful individuals understand this and hence are able to navigate life with utmost confidence and even when they face failure, they are able to come out of it quicker than others.

Decisions are intertwined and have a domino effect on our lives, they are not always obvious. Decisions decide the course of our lives. Every decision we take leads to the life we live, even unconscious decisions of what we eat, which route we take to the office, that biscuit you pop into your mouth because someone offers it at work, that impulsive purchase of a fancy gadget that is utterly useless and then the problem of how to dispose it off, that stationary cycling machine you bought which is now a clothes hanger in the middle of the living room so on and so forth all have a compound effect on how our lives are at the moment. The connection is not always clear and hence we tend to ignore the smaller decisions.

There was a Tamil movie in the early 2000s titled 12B[1]. The story was interesting, it showed the life of the hero as two stories in parallel, how his life would be if he manages to board bus number 12B to attend a job interview and what if he misses that bus on that day. The same person and how one incident can drastically change the course of life. The concept really got me interested, especially when I learnt, there may be parallel universes. My imagination ran wild thinking there was another version of me living a different life due to decisions and circumstances that rolled out differently. In the movie, when the hero boards

[1] 12B is a 2001 Indian Tamil-language romance film that was directed and written by cinematographer Jeeva; it is his directorial debut

the bus and attends the interview, he is selected and later falls in love with his boss. In the second scenario when he misses this bus, he struggles to manage finances, joins his friend's workshop as a mechanic and falls in love with another woman. But the first version is shown to evolve and become more emotionally mature than the other version. We can definitely apply this to our lives, not as parallel versions of ourselves, but the way we are today and how the 12Bs in our lives made a difference.

Small exercise to look at your 12Bs:
Take a deep breath, use this space to write down pivotal moments in your life, when the decision you took had the power to change its course. It could be that you are grateful for the right move or you regret how it turned out, or you just feel it could have turned into something greater. Just observe, **do not judge yourself**, we all have a mixed bag of decisions in life.

Exercise

The gap in our decision making is the approach, it is incomplete, based on experience alone and most of the time relies on another person's validation. So how do we fill this gap? - The answer is Holistic Decision Making.

A holistic decision is one that considers all factors of the situation and the self. There is no such thing as a perfect decision because we do not get everything we want or need, but when you take a well-informed, thought through and most importantly felt through decision, that is a holistic decision and that brings the best possible outcome on all levels of being. Even if the decision does not always give what you expected, the outcome is for your larger good and in the long run, makes complete sense.

A Holistic Decision =
(Well informed + Thought Through + Felt Through) –
(Driven by fear)

A holistic decision is not driven by fear, by guilt, by insecurities, it is not triggered by misplaced emotions. It is not a diversion from some other pressing area in life, it is a decision that empowers you, so you know that no matter what the outcome, you are 100% responsible for your life. You may notice that decisions made with this approach had far better outcomes, made you feel in charge even though external circumstances went bad, kept you grounded, brought in fresh ideas and really empowered you so that the next decision was a little better than the other. This is human evolution in its core form, as we move in life, gather experiences, are forced to make decisions, we start getting better at the decision-making game. Successful people have mastered this game.

When a decision is made with only a few parts or no parts of the holistic equation, you will feel one or more of the below:

1. It takes longer than usual for you to decide.
2. There is an internal struggle or restlessness that cannot be explained and sometimes sleepless nights.
3. The confusion seems to increase the more you think about and the more people you consult.
4. You seem to lean more towards logical arguments even when your gut feeling says otherwise.

5. You feel you have no control over the situation, are helpless and dependent on external factors.

6. There is a loss of personal power, you start blaming others for forcing you into the decision.

7. Over time when you make more such decisions, you start resigning to the fact, you have no control and then self-doubt starts to emerge.

8. At work, you start ignoring opportunities and take lesser risks.

9. Faith in your own capabilities decreases and you are unable to voice your opinion with confidence.

10. Assumption attitude arises, you assume others' perception of yourself and never clarify or have constructive dialogue.

11. Over time you start becoming a *complainer* rather than a *solution finder*.

12. Even after you manage to decide, you are not at peace, and something feels missing.

The above can be a few indicators to warn you and help you course correct. Do you feel any of the above, when you are forced into a decision corner? Are you currently feeling any of these? You are not alone, thousands struggle with this frequently and hence a strong ally can be a god sent.

Poor decision making is a result of a domino effect of hundreds of smaller decisions that are not holistic and lead to a serious condition of complacency. This is not a result of a single bad decision, it builds over years of neglect.

Complacency = Slow death

Like you voluntarily entered a quick sand and are slowly sinking to your death. It sounds extreme and gruesome but when your life starts feeling neutral, you are not really living.

It reminds me of something my school's principal, Mr Regis, told me once. He was a strict yet kind man, a maths genius who had created a niche for himself. He had taken on a huge challenge of starting his own school after he quit as a maths teacher from a reputed institution. He was in his 60s when he started the school and within no time, the school had outranked older established schools in the city. He would observe his students keenly and I was one of them. Being an active all-rounder in school, I was good at extracurriculars as well as mischief. I was also a shot put player and would attend competitions representing the school. The Principal's house was right opposite the sports stadium and at times when it got late, we would wait within the complex of his house till our parents picked us up. One such day, I was waiting alone outside his house. He was home that day and he peeked outside. He got me a children's book to read while I waited, he enquired how I was practising the sport and how my studies were going. That is when he said something which I will never forget, he said, "Do not take your gifts lightly, on judgement day God will ask you what you did with the talents & the life he gave you, that day you will need to answer him". At a young age, this did impact me, at that time, it was a fear of disappointing God and I remember thinking "Oh shit what will I answer him, am I wasting my talent and not working hard enough?". But later in life, I realised it was a deeper thought, spiritually in terms of human evolution, how am I leading this life? How am I steering it towards evolution? I started mulling over the question of what is the point of our existence.

Don't worry, we will not explore spirituality in this book, you will get an easy, fast and tested solution to take you that extra mile. Holistic decision making is the key, but what factors interfere with holistic decision making? What behaviours are keeping us stressed and confused? Turn the pages to see how seemingly harmless factors contribute to keeping us stuck in life.

2

Factors Keeping You Stressed

**"Identify and remove the weeds that are
stopping you from your true potential, they are
not as harmless as they seem".**
-Thorvi Damle

If you take away only one thing from this book, let
it be around DECISION FATIGUE, how it is
keeping you mediocre and how Tarot can be the
helping hand.

Let us go back to Gita, our developer friend from
the last chapter. She wondered why she reacted so
much to a simple question by her mother, in itself
it was harmless, but it was the last snowball added
to an avalanche that was already forming. What
Gita was experiencing was Decision Fatigue.
When questions like, what to cook and what to
wear overwhelm you, the very thought of one
more thing to decide makes you feel like you will
explode, know that you are facing decision
fatigue. It is when our brains are tired from the

thousands of decisions we are being forced to make each day, that's right we make thousands of decisions each day.

Have you noticed that as a generation, we are more restless and frustrated than our parent's generation? I am a millennial[2]; hence I am referring to the Baby boomers[2] and the early generation X[2].

When I spoke to my parents or others from those generations, I realised, pre-internet life was simpler. The internet brought a lot of ease to our lives, with everything at your fingertips in the mobile phone but it brought another nightmare hidden in the background, named "Decision Fatigue". We make more decisions in a day than ever before in history.

Think about it, say in the 1970-80s, a middle-class family in India, with the father, the earning member, with a 9-5 job (in those days it was truly 9-5, no work from home). The father would come home by 5.30 PM, relax, have a coffee, ask the kids if they were doing their homework, watch TV for an hour or so (remember TV did not have 24-hour

---

[2] Millennials - born 1981-96, Baby boomers - born 1946-64, Generation X 1965-80

channels and programmes, the news was the main programme). Dinner would be eaten with the entire family and early to bed. The choices people had in terms of what to buy, where to live, appliances and gadgets, travel and food, everything was limited, hence the decision making was limited too. A small town would have a handful of restaurants, with a limited menu, the same 10 shops in the shopping street that carried similar clothes. People visited libraries to read books, post offices to send letters and parcels, banks to withdraw money or open fixed deposits, people did not travel for leisure, they travelled to visit relatives or for pilgrimage or to attend weddings and ceremonies. The petrol bunks sold only petrol, versus today, where a petrol bunk is a mini shopping mart, selling you candy and chocolates. Since the choices and options were limited, the stress was limited and hence on average, the number of decisions were limited.

Now, look at an average day of a new age father working in the new age Technology company. His wife is also a breadwinner and works for a similar technology company. Both of them need to rush through the day, drop kids to school, make a hundred decisions on the road based on traffic and routing to reach the office on time. Similar to Gita, both of them attend meetings, respond to emails, plan and execute. They then pick up the kids, come home, and start wondering what to cook for dinner. They need to sit with the kids to complete the homework, assist in assignments and again find themselves attending late-night meetings. Most of the time, food is ordered online and by the time the kids are put to bed, both are exhausted but unable to fall asleep, scrolling on social media till 1-2 AM to repeat it all again. Added to this is the stress of planning weekends, chores, bank visits, hospital check-ups, friend catch-ups, shopping or weekend getaways. We are constantly bombarded by AI (artificial intelligence) run advertisements to buy this and that and why we need this or that to live. Constant pinging of the cell phone with messages from friends and colleagues throughout the day on chatting apps, mostly utterly meaningless forwards, videos and awkward "Hi, what are you doing?" etc.

We order home-delivered food more than any generation, and every time, we need to decide, which cuisine, which dish, which restaurant, scrolling through reviews, ratings and asking friends and family and finally deciding to order.

Travelling has become mostly to destress, which is ironic because though it is convenient and fun, the process can be harrowing. Numerous travel options and weekend getaway trends, even a small weekend trip involves a hell of a lot of coordination and planning, booking, checking the weather and it just gets worse for people with kids. Being a parent in the present generation is a herculean task, managing work, managing finances, managing relationships, managing a social life and then navigating parenthood. My silent salute to all you bravehearts battling a million decisions you need to make every single day.

According to an article in NCBI[3], it is estimated that an American adult makes 35,000 decisions a day (Sollisch 2016). They define decision fatigue as " the impaired ability to make decisions and control behaviour as a consequence of repeated acts of decision-making" The study found evidence that people experiencing decision fatigue, demonstrate an impaired ability to make trade-offs, prefer a passive role in the decision-making process, and often make choices that seem impulsive or irrational (Tierney 2011).

---

[3] www.ncbi.nlm.nih.gov/pmc/articles/PMC6119549/

It is scary but true. Most of the adult population is facing this to some degree or the other. You may ask how this affects the quality of our decisions, a valid question. When you strain a rope to its maximum capacity, it will break, similarly when we are overworked, the quality of our decisions starts to slip. If you notice, you make the poorest food choices at dinner, after a long day at work, if food is not prepared by someone else or not prepped in the fridge, you will probably order a pizza or a biryani because your brain has very little capacity left to decide on what to cook, you just give in. This may not cause any immediate harm, but patterns of eating develop and you will pay for this in the long run with health issues. This has been noticed in studies on decision fatigue, they say it causes mindless and excessive shopping at grocery stores and malls, you just cannot be bothered to pick and choose, you keep adding to your cart. If you do not have a list of items to shop for, you will end up buying a lot of things you don't actually need and at the end of the month not realise why your budget is all screwed up. Decision making is a skill and once you start relaxing the standards of quality in one aspect of life, it will spill over to all areas in life.

Decision fatigue causes us to make poor decisions on critical life issues, because we are so tired of decision making, we are less patient. We easily dismiss other's opinions and we easily give up too. If you play a game with a child and the prize is a chocolate bar, the child will be competitive till the end, a middle-aged adult might just give up midway, because the prize is not worth it. We easily cancel and postpone plans; some people have got comfortable lying or fabricating stories moving into an avoidance attitude. As a society, we are becoming more isolated, more intolerant and just extremely restless, and decision fatigue plays a role in it all. It is a vicious cycle, we may be earning more than any other generation before us, but due to decision fatigue, we outsource almost all our chores and our living expenses have skyrocketed, in turn the stress on us to earn even more.

An example stated in a study by the New York Times[4], noticed the time of a parole hearing in the jail system played an important role in the outcome. Prisoners with early parole hearing timings, were more likely to get parole than the ones later in the day and it was observed that judges may be affected by decision fatigue at the

---

[4] https://thedecisionlab.com/biases/decision-fatigue/

end of the day and hence more reluctant to approve parole.

In our daily lives, decision fatigue can affect our ability to regulate our food, exercise, sleep and affects close relationships as our interactions with them changes. The compound effect is seen in major life decisions like marriage, divorce, job change, business investments, physical and mental health issues, decisions made for children and ageing parents. I have seen pets being neglected not due to lack of love but due to decision fatigue, poor decisions made for the pets in terms of diet and medical care. Our children are not far from it, parents postpone or avoid dealing with mental health issues in children, they are unable to work with therapists, they feel they can drop off children at the therapist's office and the therapist can "fix" the issues for them. At work, we tend to make safer choices, we do not take risks. Notice, if ways of working for you have changed over the last few years versus when you began working, are you cutting corners or avoiding doing thorough QC of your work?

We cannot go back in time nor can we remove all technology and live in a grid-free zone. Though some families are choosing these drastic steps to move away and become self-sustained, it is not feasible for the majority. Is there a way to overcome decision fatigue? Is there a way to lead a balanced life and ensure our decisions are not affected by external factors, known and unknown? Yes, absolutely, but it is not a magic bean kind of solution, we cannot just "fix it", these are years of subconscious behaviours and need a lot of mindfulness and practise, over time we can definitely bring this under control.

How do we counter decision fatigue and get better at making decisions?

One of the strong methods is mindfulness or rather mindlessness. Removing our ever impatient, restless, logic-loving, seeing-is-believing mind from the equation, silencing it for a few mins through the day will do the trick. If you do not have time to meditate for an hour, no worries, steal time in your day to be mindful. What does that mean? Just stop whatever it is you are doing or thinking, close your eyes, take a deep breath and just be, observing your breathing, or the noises in your environment like the AC running, traffic in the distance, dogs barking, kids playing, anything, just hold the space of being thoughtless. There are countless apps, books, videos, guided meditations available online for free and hence I will not spend more time deep diving. Meditation need not take hours and it is not meant only for the uber-cool and spiritual people. For example, you work in an office all day, there is a window next to your seat, sometimes while you are thinking, your eyes drift to the window, you start noticing the squirrels running on the tree next to it, you see birds sitting and chirping, the leaves rustling and you are engrossed in watching them and become thoughtless for a few mins, till your desk phone rings and you come back to reality, what you did there was mindfulness meditation. The only difference is you spaced out without knowing, in mindfulness, you will deliberately space out.

We must try to remove the noise in our mind, simplify life, involve family members for decisions around the house, involve colleagues for decisions at work, and create a time slot throughout the day for calming the mind and grounding ourselves.

One of the ways to reduce decision fatigue, which I find really helpful is meal preps, creating a meal plan for the entire week, shopping only what is required for those recipes, chopping, storing vegetables, and ingredients for these recipes. So, say you shop all the groceries on Sunday morning for the week ahead, spend a few hours on Sunday chopping, pre-cooking meals and freezing them ahead of time. So that, when you reach home tired from work you will not order a pizza, instead you will pop the pre-cooked meal in the microwave and eat healthy. Another trick, I often follow is eating soaked oats for breakfast, soaking oats with fruits overnight. I feel lighter in the morning as I don't have to deal with what to cook for breakfast every morning. I save time, I eat healthy and I am full till lunch. You can apply this for your wardrobe, for your work and even for your house cleaning, scheduling the day and week ahead of time can save us from decision fatigue and you will find time in your day to meditate, go for that walk, do pranayam or just simply sit down with a cup of coffee and relax. All these are excellent tools to improve your life, but these need to be implemented, not just once, but on a consistent basis. They may not give you overnight results, but if you keep at it, you will be amazed. Like any muscle in the body, mindfulness can only be strengthened with repetition and practise. Trying the hundreds and thousands of methods available out there and finding what fits your personal needs.

Health & Pain:

The other obvious factors of stress are health, personal and family issues, financial loss etc. These are easy to identify, we all face them and overcome them in time. A person's emotional and physical states are critical in the decision-making process. There are times, people are great decision-makers at work, but are pathetic when it comes to decisions involving love and family. Decisions made when we are angry or sad or even extremely happy are not always the best for us. Similarly, when someone is in physical pain or discomfort, for example, if a person has a migraine his or her capacity to make a holistic decision is affected to a certain degree, unless they have years of practise managing their physical pain and decisions under pressure. Our armed forces are put through rigorous training and extreme physical stress to train them to be able to make decisions under pressure because, on a battlefield, a decision can make the difference between life and death and change the outcome of an entire war. To help you relate, you must have hit your foot or thumb against furniture or doors accidentally, remember the shooting pain when that happened, in the next 10-15 minutes post that injury, you are unable to even speak properly or think of anything else, pain consumes your conscious mind. We are humans after all, though we all want to believe we are superhuman. External factors and stressors play a critical role, but they are easily detected and worked on. They are obvious too when you are sick, your boss and teammates would prefer that you take the day off and come back to work refreshed, it may be because they genuinely care, but they know that a sick person may not be able to contribute towards work. Since these factors are too obvious, we will set them aside for now.

When you make holistic decisions, the outcome is not just better for you individually, it is better for everyone linked to the decision. Even if you did not have everyone's concerns in mind at that particular moment. Very often in my tarot practice, I come across families battling with the decision to move cities or even countries, with young children, spouses and parents. They are grappling with the hundreds of ways things can go right or wrong. When they use the holistic approach, they are much at peace and confident to go ahead with moving or staying. Remember, the outcome depends on each individual, what is right for you may not be right for your brother or sister or best friend.

Imagine, being able to confidently sail through life, without wasting hours and hours battling a decision internally, without wasting hours and hours discussing the issue with 10 different people adding 10 different viewpoints, none of which are helpful. Imagine, using each decision as a stepping stone to quickly climb the staircase to success. If you had the knowledge and the tools to navigate life and the multitude of decisions big or small, happy or grave enough when you need to decide to pull the plug on someone in the hospital. If you were able to bring in the same focus, clarity and confidence in all of these, you would be a force to reckon with. Your entire personality will elevate and this is what true leaders are. When you meet genuine leaders in life, you feel the awe, the admiration and the respect for them instantly, they do not demand respect, respect flows automatically and the reason is this, their ability to take decisions, tough calls under time restraints and their ability to lead and not rule. Imagine, you become the leader of your life, your family, your friends, even one person in the family with these qualities can take the entire family forward.

There are a few more factors that are not so obvious, the ones no one speaks about and the ones that hold the key to effective decision making be it in personal or business level issues. Important factors that can be game-changers just by being aware of them, those who know them, use them well but can seldom explain them to others. They can increase your chances of better outcomes almost immediately if you start taking cognisance of them and make the necessary changes to get benefits from them.

The power of a tidy space:

"The moment you start tidying, you will be compelled to reset your life"
- Marie Kondo

Not all of us can be like the Lotus plant, it grows in mud and murky waters yet manages to shoot out, like a beautiful flower with an intoxicating aroma. For the majority of us, our environments play a vital role in the way our life turns out. The spaces we live in, have a subconscious effect on our thinking, unfortunately, this is overlooked and seldom discussed. The power of our immediate environment, the bedroom, the living room, the kitchen, the office desk, even the posters on the wall are all being observed and interpreted by our subconscious mind. If this space is deliberately curated, i.e., if we take a close hard look at every item, pick and choose the space and aesthetics, we can accelerate our thinking and decision-making skills. If we let the space around us clutter, and we hoard and pile boxes, items, files and plastic, they take up premium real estate in our mind space, clogging up not just the space externally but internally too. It may sound unreal and alien in the beginning, but this is something truly successful people have noticed and used to their advantage.

Look around your space right now, if you are seated in your bedroom or office or living room, just observe, how is the space around you? What would we find, if we were to open your closet right now? Will the clothes fall all over or will we see an organised closet? How many things are stored in your attic or storage room that you haven't touched in years? Is your office desk full of papers, files, stationery and unwashed coffee mugs?

The clutter around us is part of a vicious cycle, it affects us directly yet most of the time our subconscious is creating it to distract us, which in turn clogs our mind even more and so it continues.

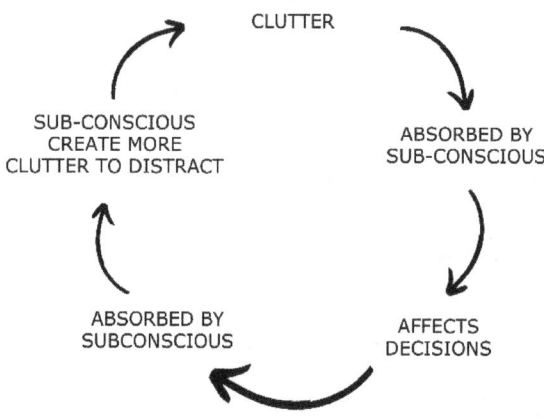

This is the reason it is so difficult to break, we are all intelligent hard-working individuals yet for 90% of us, cleaning and decluttering seems impossible, even when we manage to do it for a few days, things magically creep up again. It is observed that our mind has the ability to distract us from painful circumstances, including the pain of taking important/critical decisions. The mind is trying to protect us in its own way, and hence the subconscious creates clutter around us, the conscious brain is distracted by all the clutter and the sheer number of things around us that we bury the real, painful emotions deep within.

When the mind is avoiding having to make a decision in life, it subconsciously diverts our attention by edging us to create clutter, store and hoard stuff in our living environment, whether it is a cluttered desk at the office or a cluttered bedroom. Even if you have a fairly well-kept home/office, look deliberately through all the things you own and you will find some amount of clutter somewhere.

I have experienced this first hand, about 5 years ago, I was at one of the lowest points in life. Physically, mentally, emotionally, career-wise, just overall a very low period in life. I felt stagnant like the entire world was moving ahead and I was stuck in the same place with no way out. I was playing it safe at work, keeping my head low and just ensuring I did enough to keep my job. I had undergone my second knee surgery and faced many complications due to the anaesthesia, it was taking me longer to recover. My personal life was also stuck, and I seemed to be perpetually single. Basically, my self-esteem was low, my health was getting worse, I felt myself slipping into depression and I saw no way out. I always thank my interest in reading books, books have helped me and guided me in times like this. One such book changed my life, The Life-Changing Habit of

Tidying Up by Mary Kondo. This opened my eyes to the world of organising, and how it affects our mental space. Initially, I picked up her book because I wanted to declutter my space. I was expecting some tips and tricks on organising my closet, what I got was a peek into a whole new perspective on organising space holistically. I followed her method of holistic decluttering, i.e., keeping things that are not just functional but resonate with our energy, or in her words things that "Spark Joy", everything else was to be disposed of. I physically felt the effects of the changes, as I started donating or throwing away stuff that did not spark joy. Essentially, keeping only those things in my surroundings that brought me positive energy, apart from essential appliances of course. At the end of the exercise, which took a few weeks, I had more clarity in life, I felt lighter like some weight had been lifted from my shoulders, I could see the next steps in life and it also gave me some semblance of control over my life. I felt more confident, I was physically feeling better and motivated.

After a few days, things started moving, I noticed something shift within. I had been an impulsive shopper and post this exercise, I became a conscious shopper. Now, I will only buy something I know I will use, over time my decisions on what I bring into my space started changing. It was not even a calculated change, I never said to myself "Ok, listen we need to be a deliberate shopper", it happened organically. I try as much as possible now to keep my space clutter-free, if I let it be for a week and items pile around the house, I notice that I start getting irritated or restless.

It will now make sense to you, why successful people spend millions on interior design and creating spaces around that inspire. One of the reasons is that, they have the money to afford it, but even then, they invest in art, they invest in antiques and pieces that bring in the energy of elevation in their space. This is the reason, even office spaces are being designed with the values and thought process of the organisation in mind, a lot of thought and planning goes into creating inspiring work spaces. We all have heard of Google's out of the box and fun work environments, if you haven't yet then Google it (pun intended). You need not spend a lot of money to achieve this in your personal space, start small by decluttering which costs nothing and then anytime you buy something look at it as an investment for your space, take your time and then bring it home. I have a blog article and a podcast episode dedicated to this experience, and you can visit my website for more details.

The three factors mentioned in this chapter, awareness of Decision Fatigue, Pain or Health issues and Clutter, all need to be addressed, and all of them will require your time, effort and interest. I highly recommend giving them the due importance and acting on them as they will help you in the long run.

What do you do meanwhile? What if you have a decision to make immediately, how can you ensure it is holistic and not affected by all of the above? This is where tools come into play, tools that can empower you, aid you in critical decisions, remove the effects of decision fatigue and guide you towards the right direction, towards holistic decision making. Tarot is one such powerful tool. There are countless individuals taking advantage of tarot, getting the necessary guidance during critical and pressure-filled moments in life and not leaving anything to chance, removing any effects of decision fatigue from trickling in. You will soon be one of them, as we move through the book, but before that, you need to understand another critical key of the decision-making machine, everyone knows it, talks about it but it never gets the credit, it is due.

Stay with me to explore more…

3

Power Lies Within

"The intuitive mind is a sacred gift and the rational mind is a faithful servant".
-Albert Einstein

One afternoon, I was seated at my desk in my home office, looking outside the window, sipping my hot tea. Birds were singing and flying around on the trees and bushes outside, and suddenly I thought of a friend. I had not spoken to her in a while, and it had been ages since we met in person. As I thought about her and took my next sip, the mobile rang and I instantly knew it was her. The mobile was laid face down on the other side of the room, I walked up to it, picked it and voilà, it was in fact her calling. Has something similar happened to you? Have you predicted who was calling before you picked up the phone? Have you ever visited a place and felt eerie and all you wanted to do was leave? Have you ever just felt like someone was at the door, and opened the door before they even rang the bell? Maybe, that's just me? These are small examples of intuition in daily life and shows how easy and natural it is when we are attuned to it and for most of us this happens only when we are relaxed and in a calm state. This is because we can listen to our inner voice clearer when there is no chaos of the logical mind.

Decision making is not a stand-alone process involving the conscious mind, intuition plays a bigger role than we imagine. For most of our waking lives, we are making decisions and hence we need to start getting good at it, to increase our chance of a good life. What is required, is a balance of information and intuition, to become aware of our inner guidance system or gut feeling, one of the main parts of the holistic decision equation. Your decisions small or big will involve an element of your gut feeling and your life will start becoming easier.

Does this mean we must only listen to our gut? Are all intuition-based decisions, right? Not always, hence awareness is again critical. Using intuition, learning to interpret it and capitalising on it, is another core success skill. It is important to distinguish impulsive rash decisions based on the ego and the gut feelings from the inner guidance system. Impulsive and rash decisions always lead to regret, decisions made based on intuition do not involve regret, regret is a great indicator of analysing our past decisions. There are times we follow our heart or gut feeling, we face losses and a degree of suffering, but we do not regret it. And other times, we had a strong feeling to avoid something and we let our logical brain decide and regret going in for it.

You may be still feeling, I don't think I have an intuition, don't conclude so soon, read on.

Have you caught yourself repeating any of the below statements?

- "I knew I should not have listened to her".
- "I knew he was bad for me".
- "I knew I would find you here".
- "I knew you would love this gift".
- "I just knew this job was right for me".
- "I am glad I listened to myself even though others were saying not to do this".

These are all sentences of you having connected with your inner guidance system at some point in life. But how to regulate this? Can we channelize it to be more present, something we can see, touch, smell? Something in 3D? Absolutely, this is why humans throughout civilizations created tools and systems like the Tarot, I Ching, the

Runes, Scrying (looking into a bowl of water like Nostradamus), Pendulums etc. Astrology is one such system, but is more based on the external movements of the stars and needs intensive study of time and astronomy, it is a science. Even Numerology and Vastu shastra belong to the sciences and they require study, extensive practise and are not for everyone. These are the countless magic mirrors available for us, my preferred mirror is the tarot.

Let us understand a bit more about intuition, is it present elsewhere in nature? Yes, animals are naturally in this state, if you have a pet at home, just observe your dog or cat or bird, most of the day they are in a relaxed and present state of mind. Unless they are neglected and mistreated, our pets are chilled out, so to speak and hence they are tuned into their instincts and intuition.

I strongly believe that, if your dog dislikes a person, stay away from that person.

Animals can sense intent and hence identify threats much better and even before they occur. I read that, Elephants in a reserve in Africa can sense which vehicles are from the reserve keepers and which are from poachers, they can sense the movement of poachers versus those that care for them. They have excellent hearing capabilities but without knowing the make of the vehicles or the intent, they are able to sense who means well and who means harm, extremely fascinating.

A year ago, my brother bought a pair of lutino cockatiel birds, a mid-pandemic impulse buy. These are tiny birds originally from Australia, they are yellow in colour with bright orange cheeks, as if someone applied rouge on them. These birds weigh only 80-90 gms on average, but are intelligent, they can learn to whistle different tunes and speak a few words, they live up to 20 years if cared for properly. So, this pair of birds mated and laid their first clutch of eggs. They were first-time parents, yet, they took turns to sit on the eggs, when the female needed to rest and eat, the male would take over. Once the chicks hatched, they would feed them properly and they were so protective of their nesting box. When the chicks were old enough to come out of the box, they taught them to fly, eat and groom. All of this in 3 months, once the chicks were old enough to eat on their own, we gave them away. This pair of birds were also bred in captivity and had not seen the wild, this got me thinking, who explained to these birds what an egg is? What a chick is? Why do they need to sit on an egg? Why do they need to feed the chicks? Why do they need to teach them to fly? These tiny creatures were being guided by some force, correct? You may say, it is the hormones that lead to instincts, but to what degree can hormones pass on knowledge of raising their chicks and protecting them even from their owners? Who is managing the hormones, how does the brain of this creature know to release hormones during a particular time period? Could this be an intuition or an inner guidance system? One may argue on the dictionary meaning of the word, but a connection with a higher power, complete trust in the power and not letting the mind interfere. Letting this power guide them, to knowing more than instinctual actions, more than hormonal changes to lead a life in a certain way is intuition.

Without human interference, animals have a good lifespan depending on the species and in general lead a very present and attuned life. Just like tuning into a radio station and getting the latest news, all creatures are tuned into the guidance system of the universe and play their parts remarkably well. Humans are cursed with the mind, the forbidden fruit eaten by Eve was not just what created lust, I think it added intellect in humans and made us step away from the Garden of Eden, which is living in nature harmoniously using the inner guidance system.

Humans are remarkably intelligent and stupid at the same time, you may meet someone, who is a rocket scientist and has a great IQ, but does not know how to cook and feed himself. The industrial revolution fueled this, even more, people don't know how food is grown, children believe milk comes from plastic packets and cartons and that food is prepared in factories. This is not a problem of education per se, it is a problem of humans stepping away from their inner guidance system. How many of us can survive in the wild on our own? We would not know what is edible and what is poisonous.

Esther Hicks, an author and motivational speaker, mentions this in her talks and books: our inner guidance system is always guiding us, only if we stop and listen, we can hear. Imagine, there is a tornado warning in an area and all the people in a town are blissfully unaware, tuned into a music channel on the radio. They are going about their day, heads buried in work, inside their offices and houses. They never get the news of the tornado approaching and only realise when it is too late.

But if they had looked outside their buildings and noticed all the birds went silent in the middle of the day or noticed that the wind stopped blowing and just tuned into their inner guidance system, they could have been prepared. They would have known some major weather event was about to occur either a storm or a tornado. We humans sometimes forget that our ancestors survived a lot of natural disasters before we invented the satellites and the machines that detect cyclones and earthquakes. They were much attuned to this inner guidance system and were able to keep the species alive. With our dependency on machines and devices, literally, clinical surroundings of concrete and steel, being bombarded with information overload thanks to the internet, it is sad to see that selfie death is actually a thing. Think about it, people dying because they were too busy taking a selfie to notice they were about to fall off a cliff. Through generations of external growth and civilizations, we now need to rely on knowledge transfer through one human to another, in order to even care for our young. I know, it sounds like doomsday talk till now, like we have no hope as a species. Hold that thought, because this book is about bringing back that connection, about tuning in to the right radio station.

Many people working in the World Trade Center towers felt this the day of the plane crash on 9/11. They felt something was not right, either someone spilled coffee on themselves and got late for work or something went wrong that delayed them, like something was stopping them from going to work that day and boy were they glad they did not reach on time. This feeling and inner knowing is not activated only during stress, it is ever-present. I read somewhere that grace is always falling on us from the heavens, but we insist on holding up the umbrella. Humans are the only creatures, who have domesticated and become civilised and reached the moon, can even manipulate rain, but also managed to disconnect from their intuition. God did not send us to earth empty-handed, he gave us powers to help us survive and one of the superpowers is intuition. If we start slowly reconnecting with it, we can start deliberate living, living with intention and knowledge. Connecting with this inner guidance system will bring peace and confidence to face life, you can call it instinct, you can call it subconscious mind, you can call it telepathy, you can call it magic or you can call it a superpower, does not matter what the name is, connecting to it is important.

"It is through science that we prove, but through intuition that we discover." Henri Poincaré[5]

What about intuition in business, how much of your work decisions involve Intuition?

Ask yourself these series of questions to explore:

- Do you trust your hunches, when confronted by an important decision?
- Do you feel in your body, if a decision is right or wrong?
- Do you put a lot of faith in your initial feelings about people and situations?
- Do you put more emphasis on feelings than data, when you make a decision?
- Do you rely on your gut feelings, when dealing with people?
- Does your intuition often turn out to be right all along?
- Do you trust your experience when arriving at reasons for making a decision even if you can't explain why?
- Do you keep your intuitions close to your chest? If so, why?

---

[5] French mathematician, physicist and astronomer

Are you surprised by your answers? These series of questions[6] were asked to C-level executives and most of them answered yes, they rely on their intuition.

We all have made, are making and will need to make decisions in life. The decisions may be C-suite level or day to day decisions, but we all need to make them and intuition play a significant role.

Jay Liebowitz[7] describes intuition as a combination of analytics and instinct. It is experience driven, holistic, affective, quick, and non-conscious. And including intuition in the decision-making process, can be extremely valuable, if approached in the right manner.

A good example is hiring a new employee, apart from the resume or any references from the previous employer, hiring a new person for a job is one decision where gut feeling and intuition plays a major role. You have limited time in an interview and even with multiple interviews and tests, in the end your decision time is limited. Many managers end up hiring the person based

---

[6] The Intuitive Executive, E.Sadler-Smith & Shefy, Academy of Mgt Executive , 2004

[7] Author of Bursting the Big Data Bubble: The Case for Intuition-Based Decision Making

on their intuition, within the first five minutes of an interaction. I have experienced this, when I was working in corporate, even before the interview stage, I would be required to shortlist candidates based on their resumes or LinkedIn profiles. Within the first few minutes, I was able to identify the best fit for the interview. These decisions were experience-driven, my mind had the past experience of reading through profiles, they were holistic, because my mind was searching for keywords within the resume and also trying to find connections with the job description, and it was doing this quickly and non-consciously. Similarly, decisions made on dating apps, on marriage websites while sifting through profiles, or decisions of hiring a maid, or even mundane decisions of buying a gift for a friend involve intuition.

A study[8] conducted at Tel Aviv University in 2012, found that when top executives were forced to choose between two options based on instinct alone, the participants made the right call up to **90% of the time**.

---

[8] The results of this study were published in the journal PNAS.

Intuition is not a new fad word; it is our natural guidance system to ensure the best survival scenarios. Although, there is a downside to it, decisions made with what is underdeveloped intuition, don't always have a positive result. Our intuition may not always be strong enough and we may mistake restlessness or impulsiveness for intuition. We have poor intuition especially outside of our comfort zone. If you have worked in a domain for many years, your intuition-based decisions will be bang on, but if your company asks you to take on new projects outside your domain, you may not have the great intuition to support your right decisions. Intuition needs to be developed and sustained, though it is naturally present in all, learning to identify it takes practise.

Peter Drucker, one of the fathers of management said "I believe in intuition only if you discipline it".

What is the solution then? The solution is bridging the gap and becoming a rational intuitive decision-maker. Gather your facts and check-in with intuition, before you take that final step.

Let us look at a non-business example. If you are hiring a babysitter, check for references, do background verification with trusted websites or local law enforcement, ask for identity documents, ask questions on how they will handle the child in a situation etc. Then check in with what was your instinct when they first walked in, did you feel safe with this person in the room? How did they speak or move or dress? Then take your decision. They say, maternal instincts are very strong and when a woman becomes a mother, these are naturally in a heightened state, an in-built mechanism to keep offspring safe.

Why are we unable to connect to our intuition at times? All the factors we discussed earlier are the reason, information overload, being bombarded by distractions and temptations every few minutes, our attention is pulled into ten different directions and we are unable to stay focused, decision fatigue is very real and if we have added factors of illness or cluttered space, imagine the pressure on our internal thinking conscious mind. Intuition then just gets ignored as a tiny annoying voice and unless we change our ways, bring meditation and mindfulness deliberately into our daily schedule, have stricter regimes and plan ahead, there is very little that can help us improve this skill. If we cannot hear our own thoughts, how can we hear the inner voice? Yet there is hope, I believe we can not only manage it, but we can also master it. We are closing in on the magic mirror, very soon you will have a tangible tool to achieve this state, you need to keep turning the pages of this book.

As an exercise, think if you have a story of intuition in your life, or have heard of a story from somewhere, if you love animals, are there more examples of living in tune with nature, observing your own pets, or observing the crows and squirrels and sparrows outside your windows, the ants that create magnificent ant hills and we barely notice them. Talk to your parents or spouses or even young children and find if they have a story or an incident triggered by intuition. As we open up to more human, animal and nature-centric interaction, we will identify incidents in life when we did trust our intuition and it paid off. When did trusting your gut help you in a situation in life?

You must be wondering, what has all of this got to do with tarot? Tarot is that tool that can channel this intuition, this inner guidance system. It can tap into this critical energy source and easily interpret the messages. The next chapter will unlock the door to this tool, handing you the information you need to elevate your life. The aim is not to make you a tarot reader, it is to empower you to explore this tool that so many are already benefiting from. We will dive straight into this in the next chapter, you are now equipped with the necessary information on decision-making and hence earned the code to pass through.

4

How Tarot Can Transform Your Life?

"Tarot is that magic mirror on the wall that insists on showing you what you cannot see or at times what you refuse to see."
- Thorvi Damle

How tarot can transform your life:

The need of the hour is a support system for individuals to take the right next steps in life. Though the modern world has all the external luxuries we can imagine, yet most of us are battling our problems alone. Friends, family and mentors can only do so much and most of what they advise is from their own life experiences, it is not holistic. You are the only person who knows what is good for you if only you could listen intently to yourself. It may sound like a cliche, but it is like the famous saying "If you give a man a fish, you feed him for a day. If you teach a man to fish, you feed him for a lifetime"(Source Google). People may help you on occasional decisions in life, but if you can get better at it, you will be more independent.

Does this mean you have to learn tarot? Not at all, you only need to know what it is, you need not learn it or practise it. As you work with your tarot practitioner for a few sessions and decisions, you will start becoming more aware of your inner world, your intuition and your subconscious patterns, eventually you will not need tarot or any other tool. You will NOT become dependent on tarot for each decision, instead, tarot will force you to look at issues from a different angle and your inner intelligence will slowly take over.

For example, if you approach a tarot practitioner for a question on your career, you have a micromanaging boss who is constantly harassing you, the cards advise you to be patient, practise self-restraint in your thoughts and actions, not to take things personally because, in a few months, you will get another opportunity. You follow the advise, you will become calmer, you will learn to distance yourself internally from blames and problems, you will see the power of silence, your boss will notice the changes in you and will get a bit scared, as you are acting more in control of yourself and he is unable to get a reaction from you. In a few months, you do receive another opportunity and move on without all the internal drama. Do you think this life lesson of self-control was only applicable for that particular situation? This is a life lesson you will not forget, because you worked hard on learning it, and in any situation in the future, your personality has now been upgraded to include self-control, you practise it long enough and it will become a part of your nature. A similar situation occurs in the future, you will be ready to handle it and will not need to consult tarot. The key though is action, working on the advice given, inaction will not move anything.

ATTENTION - These stories you are about to read, are meant to showcase how tarot helped guide in a situation, the outcomes do not matter. I am not promoting a 10 day get rich sort of plan, so these are not your typical success stories. These are inspired by real clients; I have worked with and who have graciously agreed to be part of this book. The names and references have been changed to maintain their privacy, but the learnings are included.

Remember, there is no blanket good or bad decision for anyone, I would encourage you to look at this from the angle of analysis of the questions, and the answers rather than judging the decisions taken. What is right for you may be wrong for me. I invite you to walk in the shoes of these individuals for a few minutes, as you read their stories and experience tarot through their eyes.

What you will NOT find in the stories, is drastic life-changing outcomes. I believe tarot should become part of life, not a once in a lifetime prediction that changed your life. I want tarot to be a consistent friend, philosopher and guide in life's journey. So, I will apologise for the lack of sensational overnight success stories, these are real people with real lives and tarot helped them one decision at a time.

Please note through the rest of this book by Seeker, I mean the person asking the questions in a tarot reading and by the practitioner, I mean the tarot reader. I am using the term practitioner instead of reader because I believe tarot cards should not be read, they should be analysed (Inspired by Benebell Wen's book *Holistic Tarot*).

Rishabh's Dilemma:

Rishabh had resigned from his job recently. He was 40 years old, married with two children and ageing parents who lived with him. His wife was working too, but her income was enough to cover the basic necessities alone. He did not have another offer in hand, but this decision seemed to be coming from deep within. He had worked hard in this company, given more than 10 years of his life to it, he had built a team from scratch and implemented processes and structures within the company that helped them grow. Over the past year or so, he noticed changes in the way in which he was being treated, the management had become cold and more distant. The priorities of the company were shifting and they were focusing more on money and less on their people. In doing so, the management had started compromising value systems and the culture of the company, which Rishab had worked so hard to develop and sustain. The pandemic was still wreaking havoc and job uncertainty was looming high. When he came to me, he had mixed emotions and wanted to understand more the effects of his decision. He wanted to know his prospects of finding a new job at the same time, he wanted to know if this company would try and retain him. He wanted to understand how this would affect his family and dependents and if this was a rash decision.

We discussed briefly and I started pulling cards for his questions. Disclaimer: I do not read cards,

I interpret them depending on the questions and my intuition. There are general meanings associated with the cards that one can find on google, but they are not the only meanings of the card.

Question one- Was this decision rash? Will I regret it later?
The cards indicated that this was indeed a good decision at this point for him. This was not a rash decision, this was intuition-based and he would get good results later. The main cards that popped indicated success, recognition and improvement in life circumstances.

Question two - Will the existing company try and retain me? Will they realise they mistreated me and that they are losing a good asset?

Definitely, he will feel that justice is served or that balance is restored, but this is more of a temporary victory that will not bring inner satisfaction. He needs to refocus and let go, as he is moving towards something bigger in life. The existing company may offer him something to try and retain, or may wish him good luck and let him go, but they will feel the pinch or loss of him as a good asset. Either way, this will not be a great winning moment for him personally, so he should start focusing on moving ahead. This decision will help him as well as the company's management to refocus on what is important, and a win-win situation on both sides.

Question three - What are my future prospects? What is holding me back?

The cards indicated that things will look up soon and he will be motivated to act, start looking for a job with rigour. It may take up to 7 months, so patience is required as at this stage in his career, he needs the right job, not any job. His inner fears are stopping him. He needs to have faith in himself, he should apply for jobs even if he feels he is not well equipped. He needs to develop faith in his own abilities and aim, higher than usual in terms of roles. His emotional state is critical for his success, if he observes and manages his emotional state, he can achieve much more. He should focus on bringing balance emotionally, deal with internal fears by taking practical steps and move ahead with hunting for the right job, one step at a time. Even if someone offers him a pay cut, he should look at the job profile and decide based on the job profile, financial growth will follow once he pushes his limits on the role. I had pulled the page of pentacles which had indicated a new beginning but on a smaller scale.

At this point Rishabh was taken aback, he had not shared with me a fact. He had an offer from a start-up for a role that would require a lot of work and bigger responsibility but was paying less. This role would give him a chance to set up a company culture from the beginning, build and lead a workforce with values. He was still undecided on if this was a good option for him.

Overall, the conclusion of the session was this, Rishabh should believe in himself, trust this decision and move ahead. It may take longer than usual, but he would find the right role for him. He should focus more on the role rather than compensation at this point. Irrespective, if his current company offers him something for retention, he needs to focus on growth and movement. He would have better control of his work and finances in the coming year, he would have clarity and passion for his work. He would be a leader and people would look up to him for guidance and solutions. The advice was to stay grounded, balance emotions and make slow progress like a bull or a rhino, both these animals cannot be intimidated easily, they decide their own pace. They can choose to stand still and no one can budge them or they can run at speeds no one can catch them, bottom line they usually maintain a slow but steady pace of movement. He needed to do the same in his career, and he would go places. He also needed to push himself out of his comfort zone and apply for roles he thought he was not ready for.

He walked away with validation for his questions, more confidence and enthusiasm for the future. The session helped him refocus and showed him his blind spots or things to be aware of. In a few weeks, his current company offered him a promotion and agreed to make changes in ways of working. As a result, he could think of more investment opportunities for his finances and the working culture of the company improved with the changes implemented. A win-win situation as we had discussed earlier. The key is he continued to follow the advice and irrespective of the choice he made, the clarity he gained boosted his confidence.

Remember, you are creating your own future, as a tarot practitioner, I can only guide you, action needs to be taken in order for you to reap the benefits. I have had clients who have refused to take action and decided to ignore the warnings, they have suffered from their decisions. The cards indicated that if they took measures to avoid the pitfalls, they would be successful. They interpreted this as they will be successful no matter what and later had the rude awakening that action is required. Nothing will move in life if you do not lift a finger.

Tarot can help a lot with career and workplace-related questions and challenges. It can give you an edge over your competition and help understand your priorities. It can help you guide on where to focus at a given point in time for maximum growth.

Clara's fears:

Clara had moved to a new city, she was on the verge of a massive life change. She had divorced recently and her only daughter was with her ex-husband, as she herself was not yet financially independent. She moved to a new country for a fresh start. She and her ex-husband had both planned to eventually move to this new country and now here she was all alone. She was missing her daughter and she wanted to get a stable job and prove herself as a capable parent. She reached out to me for a session, she had a lot of questions about her future.

Question: Will she be able to find a good job?

The cards showed she would find a job, but they actually revealed something she had not shared with me. They revealed a lover, a suitor who was interested in her and who could bring stability in her life. She was surprised that this came up.

Tarot cards in my experience reveal what is most on your mind, subconscious mind. On a surface level, you may choose to focus on one area, but the underlying area always gets revealed. For her, it was this brand-new relationship, the cards revealed a loving, caring and supportive person. He would be a support system more than the job itself. She would find a job but the focus right now was this supportive relationship. The lovers card and two of cups along with the King of cups revealed emotional happiness, and stability.

Question: Will she get custody of her daughter?

The cards revealed that she may not immediately get full custody of her daughter. But she would be able to get joint custody and this would be in favour of her daughter. The pentacles cards showed that her ex-husband was a good father, and hence this would be better for the child. She agreed that her daughter was attached to both of them and it would be fair for her to have both parents accessible.

Clara left the session full of hope and at ease, looking forward to a better tomorrow.

In a few weeks, I was pleasantly surprised to get the news that she had married this new love and the very next year was blessed with a child. Her ex-husband moved to this new country with her daughter and she was able to enjoy joint custody. This was not the only consultation; Clara continues to include tarot in her times of doubt to help her make better decisions in life. If one is happy in their personal life the external can be handled easily. Times when your support system is taken away or shaken, you can start questioning your identity and times like these, tarot can be that person you rely on, to cheer you on and assure you of hope. Remember, it is only a mirror, it is reflecting the intelligence hidden within you.

Soniya's restlessness:

Soniya had been served a divorce notice and had been running pillar to post trying to find a good lawyer to represent her in court. Her husband had planned this secretly with his family for months and suddenly moved to his hometown, leaving behind his wife and his young son. He had sent her the notice through the post and falsely accused her of mistreating and torturing him in the marriage. Soniya had been expecting a separation, but the manner in which it unfolded had disturbed her. He was demanding divorce but had not even mentioned his son anywhere in his petition. He wanted to wash his hands off them, yet hurt her in the process it seemed. She had recently moved back to India from the US and was desperate to move back there. She had a stable job and was able to financially support her son, but this new legal battle was uncharted territory. She had found a lawyer who seemed alright, but she didn't fully trust him as she had been conned by two others for money before this. She came for a tarot session because she wanted to know about her prospects of moving abroad and also understand about the divorce. She also had a family wedding coming up and she was tense about attending it and meeting all her relatives who would bombard her with questions about her divorce.

Question: Possible outcome of the divorce.

The cards indicated that she would need to practise utmost restraint and inner strength over the next couple of months. There would be a situation created to provoke her and push her to explode and react in anger. This would be a planned attempt to prove that she was a verbally abusive spouse. This was going to be a test in life that could potentially evolve her or cause her harm depending on her level of restraint. She initially assumed it was going to be at the wedding she would attend. But it was not that, I clarified that this would be at the upcoming first court hearing during the court-appointed counselling session. Soniya had one weakness and that was her temper, she was not someone who was constantly yelling or upset, she was a happy person, but her husband knew which buttons to push and she had been tested with her temper, even if she was morally and ethically right in her arguments, her temper could harm her more than getting her point across.

The Strength card was pivotal in this reading, like the girl in the card image softly taming the lion, she too had to tame the beast within, not just with brutal force i.e., willpower was not sufficient, she had to look at the larger picture and give up the need to be proven right. The Five of Swords and the Tower indicated this pivotal moment, though they are cards of strife and worry, in this reading they were challenges she had the potential to overcome and evolve.

Question - What are my prospects of returning to the US?

She definitely would get chances but in the next year around summertime. She had to be patient and wait, these opportunities would suddenly come up to her. The cards advised her to be patient and keep looking, keep applying but not with extreme force, take her time and keep her avenues open. She should network and keep her resume active and she would definitely get opportunities. Her priority was to deal with some life lessons, this is what made circumstances bring her back to India, and once she faced them, she would be free to move back.

Soniya felt reassured after the reading. She was able to move away from her victim mode and have more control over her life. She was still a bit stressed with the upcoming encounters with her family and husband. Her trip to the family wedding was successful and uneventful, she managed to keep the questions at bay and enjoy the wedding. She was tested to her core during the court session, she managed to overcome her weakness and she held her tongue as well as the body language. She was calm, composed and unhinged by the various allegations her husband made sitting right opposite to her in the counselling session. She did not interrupt and despite various provocative statements, she spoke only when the counsellor asked for her side of the story. She kept it short and smart, and it was clear to the counsellor as to whose side had the truth, the same was reflected in the notes.

Post this her confidence soared, the next court session was a breeze compared to this and her lawyer turned out to be excellent at presenting the rest of her case. She later connected with me and shared that she had not expected the cards to read her mind like this and the heads-up on inner control helped her case tremendously. She also consulted an astrologer a few weeks later, who confirmed that things would change after summer in terms of her US travel.

You would have noticed in all the examples till now, tarot was only holding the mirror, these are smart, educated, hardworking and intelligent people, so you may feel that the insights should be something they should have known. But life does not work that way, when we are in the middle of a crisis, hit by the unexpected turn of events, when we have responsibilities weighing us down and still, we need to get up and work every day, when we are being disturbed by external factors like health issues, work pressure, peer pressure, family feuds and even daily pressures of traffic, managing the home, grocery shopping, adding to all of these the last 2 years dealing with changes due to the pandemic, it can be a lot. Life is always crystal clear in hindsight, when we look back at our situations after 2-3 years, we can judge ourselves harshly and say why didn't I see this? Remind yourself, in reality, you do not have 20/20 vision in the present moment, we all need mirrors in the form of friends, family, guides, mentors and even their advice is skewed, based on the bias of knowing us. *The only person who can guide you is you, and the tool to help you listen to you is tarot.*

Tarot & Relationships:

I have helped many clients who were confused with new romantic relationships. Some of them were being breadcrumbed i.e., to be led on with very little communication or conveniently kept in a friendzone and confused. The cards helped them identify red flags they had chosen to ignore. I never pull cards about the other person in a relationship without the consent of the other person. For me, relationships start with you, and what you bring into the relationship can predict the outcome of it, and by this, I mean the self-worth and self-love you bring in, not how much you do externally for the other person. We live in denial many times and we stop giving ourselves the love in the relationship. My clients were able to make decisions, have discussions with their partners and either go different ways to find someone better to work on their relationship with open conversations with the other.

Tarot can help you identify deeper aspects to a relationship and the outcome predicted is purely dependent on the decisions and work one is ready to put in. For example, for one of my clients, she had started dating this colleague at work. He would flirt with her a lot in the beginning and slowly they started talking every day and sharing more and more with each other. He liked her but he did not expect things to evolve so soon, he was a nice guy but he got confused and started finding excuses to quarrel and break the relationship. He would at times show interest and at times act cold. She was stressing out over this and she didn't know what to do. She liked him and she genuinely hoped this would evolve into a serious relationship and eventually to marriage. He introduced her to his parents and that encouraged her to believe he was interested too, but then he raked up fights and blamed her for being immature. When she came for the reading she wanted to know if this relationship would last. The cards revealed that this would end in heartbreak, they revealed that he was more focused on his career, something she had not shared with me. He was actually preparing for exams to pursue higher education and would eventually have to move cities. The cards revealed that they were not compatible and contradictory to her belief, she was more mature than him. She was taking her chances and trying to explore this relationship. The cards also revealed that her personal insecurities kept attracting the wrong guys. She was beautiful but believed she was not good enough. She needed to work on her self-worth and she was advised to break this off soon. Further, the cards advised her to take a break from dating for a year and focus on her inner stability. She had to focus on self-respect, self-love, and grounding her energies. She was advised to volunteer, and do some service-oriented work, meets youngsters involved in service and try to elevate her circle with people who had a purpose in life. The relationship ended soon after this, she did face heartbreak but she did not follow through on the advice that could have accelerated her healing. She did not take a break from dating, she eventually did for a few months and she developed her spiritual and meditation routine, she worked on her self-worth. After a few years, she has now found the right match for her and is getting married soon.

Free will plays a huge part in this, approach tarot only for guidance, it cannot fix your issues for you and it cannot predict what will happen. It can warn you of the most plausible outcome, based on the current state of affairs. For example, if Joshua has a job offer from a prestigious firm, he is happy in his current job and this offer was unexpected as he was not looking out actively to change his job. He is confused, about whether to accept it or not. In his current job, he has a clear path to promotion and an exciting project, but the other firm is well known and offers better pay. Say, he consults a tarot practitioner and the cards reveal heartbreak with the new job, that if he takes it on, he will have a lot of challenges. Joshua can still opt to join the new firm and face these challenges head-on, it is completely his free will and his choice. As I mentioned, there is no right or wrong decision per se, there are only decisions that can lead you faster towards your growth and destiny. Joshua may end up working 2 years extra for the promotion, but he will still learn his life lessons.

Most issues arise from the deep unconscious and unlike popular thought, everything is interrelated. Your love life will affect your work-life on some level. If you have what you need in all areas of life, you are generally happy in life and don't have major concerns, you will have better chances of success and making the right decisions for you.

How can you incorporate tarot in your life?

I would recommend first, reading this book till the end, it will equip you with all the basic information before you proceed.

1. You can then review and pick a good tarot practitioner.
2. Start with a reading around any one area of your life and remember it is not one-way traffic, the discussion should be two ways.
3. Avoid 10-15 min reading sessions or readings over email or recorded videos, a voice call or one-to-one session minimum of 30 minutes is recommended.
4. Give time post sessions to observe changes within you.

5. Keep track of the outcomes and for a year at least involve tarot in your life decisions, need not be pivotal or life-changing, why wait till you are under tremendous stress.

Below are a few common questions where you can involve tarot:

1. Should I change my job or my domain?
2. Should I invest in a course or higher studies to increase my chances of getting a job?
3. Should I invest in this venture? Should I include this in my services/product portfolio?
4. Is this a suitable person to enter into a business partnership? Are we on the same wavelength? Do we have similar core values?
5. What are my chances of moving abroad? Should I be focusing on this right now? Should I invest in this agency that helps people move abroad?
6. Where is my relationship headed? Are we compatible for marriage?
7. Why is the relationship with my parents strained? Can I improve this and how?
8. What is blocking my promotion? What should I focus on right now?

9. I am feeling restless, is this a mid-life crisis? What can I do to channelize my energy better?

10. Should I invest in this property? Should I sell my property right now?

11. Are there chances to reconcile with my friend or family member?

12. Should I stay or divorce? What are the pros and cons?

13. What is the likely outcome of my legal issue? Is there something I am unable to view?

14. Should I have the conversation now with my boss about my promotion or project move?

15. How will my health be in the next few months? Will I find the right cure for my illness? What is the underlying emotion behind my illness?

16. Should I adopt a new pet?

17. How is my divorce affecting my child? How can I better support my child?

Basically, there is no limit to the questions you can ask the cards, as I mentioned it is of no use wanting to know about your ex or your enemies. Tarot is a self-development tool and yes children below 18 and aged parents or anyone who is completely dependent on you is something tarot can help with, but for everyone else, the angle to approaching the interpretations is only for you as an individual. It does not reflect on how good or bad the other person is.

Exercise: Think of five questions, most prominent in your head right now. Which five questions, if answered, will improve your life right now? Write them down in the box below and then number them based on priority. This could be a new beginning of your journey with tarot. But before you hurry on to search for a tarot practitioner, ensure to finish this book. The next chapter will serve as a traffic signal handbook, remember when you gave your driving test, a day before you sat down and tried to memorise all the traffic signs and posts. Well, this is your handbook of signals to help you make most of your investment in tarot, both money and time.

Exercise

5

BUSTING MYTHS & Sneak Peek Into A Tarot Session

"Remember that the Tarot is a great and sacred arcanum - its abuse is an obscenity in the inner and a folly in the outer. It is intended for quite other purposes than to determine when the tall dark man will meet the fair rich widow."
-Jack Parsons

Busting myths about Tarot:

Tarot has been misunderstood and misinterpreted through centuries. It has been associated with witchcraft, sorcery, magic, con artists, psychics and some of the religions have banned it as they deem it as evil, the work of the devil.

In recent times, movies and web series depict the tarot used by con artists or characters that are comical and ridicule the art of tarot. The stigma attached to it is large and most of us do not even want to try it out lest we are ridiculed or associated with any of the above titles. Personally, I am fascinated by all esoteric arts and hence I am comfortable with these terms, except con artist of course. All these areas of study have their own importance and place in our world, but science claims to be the authority on reality and fake. Science, unfortunately, does not consider that there is a lot about humans and universal consciousness that is yet to be discovered and measured. I am a student of science, having a background in chemistry and biotechnology. I too was apprehensive about tarot, in the beginning, I was intrigued with it and at the same time felt it was too wishy-washy. The only experience I had was that of watching tarot readings on YouTube, the ones on YouTube are mainly for entertainment purposes, these are mass readings i.e., made for a large number of people and hence similar to the horoscopes in the newspaper are not accurate. As I researched more, a new side of tarot came to light and my fascination deepened.

As Benewell Wen states in her book "Holistic Tarot", tarot is a tool, and a tool by itself cannot be good or bad. It can be used by people with good or bad intentions. For example, a knife can cut a cake and also be used to stab someone that does not make the knife evil. Similarly, tarot is a deck of cards with beautiful imagery and it can be used by genuine practitioners as well as fake ones, they can be collected just for their art or used to practise divination, they are also used in manifestation of techniques.

It is sad that myths and wrong beliefs are hindering people from benefiting from tarot. It is my attempt to give you as much information as possible so that you approach it as an analytical tool.

Listed below are a few common myths:

- Tarot is created by the devil.
- Tarot is just a scam used to deplete your bank balance.
- Tarot can predict your future.
- Tarot can only be read by psychics and clairvoyants.
- Tarot is passed on from one generation to another, and hence you cannot learn it.
- Tarot is practised by gypsies, magicians, witches and wizards in dark rooms, with velvet curtains, a huge crystal ball, at the end of shady allyes.

- Tarot cards are always right, once they predict it will happen.
- Receiving the Death card means someone will die.
- Tarot is used to curse or put a spell on someone, it is a tool for black magic.
- Tarot reading can bring bad luck to your life.
- Tarot can help me spy on my ex.
- Tarot can help me bring back my ex.
- Tarot can help me read the minds of others.

These are just some of the popular myths, there are many more out there.

Important to note: Anyone who preys on your vulnerability cannot be a good tarot practitioner.

If you receive messages saying things like:

"Spirit asked me to message you" or "The universe has a message for you" beware, these are frauds. As I said, you should feel like asking the questions, no one should instil fear in you to go for a tarot reading. I experienced this myself a few weeks ago, someone with a credible-looking Instagram account messaged me using the app, she started by saying "Spirit would like to do a reading for you, there is a message for you from above." I politely declined saying, "I did not want a reading as of now." She continued by saying, "Spirit led me to you because there is a blessing coming your way and there is some bad energy stopping it from being yours already". I clearly stated again that thank you, but I am not interested in any tarot reading from her, she continued messaging me "Now the spirit's voice is getting louder...". She clearly was trying to instill fear, create anxiety, curiosity and extract some money from me. People like these are contributing to tarot being seen as a farce. Fear-mongering is not something a true tarot practitioner will indulge in, ever. Like any other field, one needs to be a bit skeptical while approaching tarot, the skeptic in you will ask more questions and will help you get more from the reading. When you are approached by people with getting rich quick schemes or that Nigerian prince who is ready to share his fortune with you, but needs you to first transfer X amount to his account, it is your common sense and research that will help you find the right tarot practitioner for you.

What does a tarot session look/feel like?

Many of you reading this book have not experienced a tarot session and even for those who have, the next section will provide some general guidelines of what to expect before, during and after the session. Like with other tools, tarot is not for everyone, it is definitely not for people looking for quick fixes in life. Tarot would suit you if you have a hunger to excel in life, if you plan ahead or would like to plan ahead, set goals, have a vision (can be in any area in life), or someone aspiring to be all of this.

Things to consider before a reading

- Tarot does not belong to any religion, cult or witchcraft, it is an independent tool and one can connect with any deity, angel, universal energy or higher power. It is very personal in that sense.
- Tarot may not always give you a Yes or No, it will help you weigh your options, you will need to make the choice in the end.
- Tarot will help you understand the energies and the outcome of the situation in question.
- Tarot taps into your subconscious so it is imperative to phrase and hold your questions in your mind as clearly as possible.
- Sometimes, you may be asking about situation A, but your subconscious is focused

on situation B, the reading will answer for situation B, which is good, as it helps pinpoint the underlying condition.

- Future predictions are never fixed, we are the creators of our reality and Tarot will show you what the outcome will be if you continue on the present path.
- Refrain from asking about another person without his/her consent, especially Ex-partners or other adults. It violates the sanctity of the reading. As a parent of a minor, you may ask about the child.

Things to consider after a reading

- Post the reading; follow the guidance that may be channelled through. Action is required on some level (Physical, mental, emotional) to achieve your desired results.
- Please find a quiet place and time to go through what is discussed, things may pop up in your subconscious and you need to be silent to grasp these indications.
- Do not analyse the cards, the interpretations are not always the same. So, if you google the tarot card meaning you may be disappointed, and just by referencing the card meanings, one should not attempt a reading for another person.

- Have faith and allow time to take its course, instead concentrate on the actions you need to take.

A typical tarot session:

Every tarot practitioner has his/her own style, so I cannot speak for everyone. The below description is what I practise as well as what I have observed other practitioners do as well.

I usually ask my clients to share their name, latest photograph and date of birth before the session. These help me focus during my meditation session. I meditate before each session, concentrating on the client's energy and sometimes I see visions that may give more insights into their issues and I feel their emotions too. These types of intuitions are called Clairvoyance (seeing images) and Clairsentience (recognizing feelings), others may hear voices (Clairaudience) or have an inner knowing (Claircognizance). These are heightened naturally in a few people, others can develop them over time with spiritual and meditative practices.

Clients may choose to share their area of query before the session, but if not, that is also fine. I prefer voice calls to connect with clients, this way they can choose their quiet corner at home or at the office for the session. Not all clients can travel to meet me in person and I have clients overseas as well. I ask clients to find a peaceful corner where no one will disturb them, spend at least 5 minutes in silence or meditation before we connect. I also encourage them to write down the questions so there is clarity before we begin.

Once we connect, we discuss the details, I allow them to share whatever they are comfortable sharing. If needed I ask for further information, the cards will reveal them anyway. Post this, I decide on the spread that would be relevant. A spread means the order in which I will lay out the cards, and each card position will signify something. A basic spread is a three-card spread, signifying past, present and future. For example, If the client wants to ask about their relationship, I shuffle and pull three cards and lay them out beside one another. The first card indicates the recent past, the second card indicates the present, and the last card indicates the recent future. There are hundreds of card spreads and sometimes one may not need any particular card spread. If the cards I pull do not give me enough information, I shuffle and pull clarifier cards, or more cards to get a better insight.

Photo 1: Three Cards Spread[9]

The discussion begins post this and I keep sharing the photos of the cards with the clients, so they can follow along. It is important for them to see the cards, they are able to relate better and sometimes share what stands out in a card for them. Remember, this is about how the client views the image so their input is required. For a proper guidance session, I always recommend spending at least 40-60 minutes. Somehow, I do not advocate 10 minutes readings, especially for life-altering decisions.

---

[9] **Photo Credits:** Cesar Raj photos Pondicherry

Supportive cards:

Oracle cards are also used in conjunction with tarot cards to get more information. Unlike tarot cards, oracle cards do not have a set structure, they are free-flowing and artistically depicted. They usually contain messages either on the card itself and/or contain a reference booklet. Similar to the tarot cards, oracle cards are shuffled and pulled out and then the practitioner interprets them either through intuition alone or uses the booklet to read the given meaning.

Oracle cards have imagination as their limit, you will be taken aback by the beautiful and striking artwork in some of them, and they do inspire our intuitive brain. I use them for the advice part of the session as the booklets provide a straightforward message. Oracle cards are something anyone can use, if you are interested go through the many options online, buy one deck, and practise pulling a card from it each day, slowly you will align with the deck itself and it can be your personal divination tool.

When I mention aligning with a deck, the imagery on it must resonate with you. There were a few tarot & oracle decks I just could not resonate with and I either gave them away or resold them.

Confession - I am an avid collector of tarot and oracle cards and guard them like Gollum from the Lord of the Rings "My precious"!!

Once the questions are discussed, advice shared and inputs digested, I may suggest alternative remedies or aides that help with the inner balance. My preferred aides are crystals, I work extensively with them and have seen results. Depending on the requirement, I suggest crystal pendants, bracelets or raw stones. These are not mandatory, but if something can help relieve the stress and align to the goal, I believe there is no harm in trying. My clients who have invested in crystals have experienced the aide. There are many other such tools or small rituals that can help us refocus, remove external noise and calm our senses. Less is more and even one or two of these suggestions if applied regularly have a lot of impacts.

First-hand experience is always the best teacher. Test out the waters yourself, give tarot a chance. The above information is to ensure you have some basic knowledge and can ensure you are not taken advantage of. It will also help you take more control of the tarot session itself. This side of tarot is still evolving and there aren't many practitioners who approach it this way. Most of them still focus on fortune-telling and I do not blame them, we all have the allure to know our future and indulging in such readings from time to time, helps us feel more hopeful in life. But when it comes to deliberate living, we need to dig a bit deeper.

I will share some of the tarot cards that have archetypal interpretations and at first glance appear difficult to read, some of these have got tarot a bad rep and as you read through you will hopefully see them in a different light. This is not a list of all the cards, I have handpicked a few so that you have a sneak peek into the world of tarot and how it relates to our internal world and psyche.

What does tarot mean to me?

Tarot has empowered me beyond words. Growing up, I was an intuitive and curious child, I would connect easily with animals and even plants. My mother recalls I would talk to the flowers in our terrace garden and when two flowers bloomed in adjacent pots, I would introduce them to each other. I would also talk to the sun and pick up stray animals from the streets and bring them home, which was a headache for my parents. Imagine, when I was around 10-11 years old, I brought home a cow I found wandering the street (a common sight in India) and tied it to my gate, when evening fell, the cow easily pulled itself free and walked home. I felt really sad, I could not see the starving condition of that cow. Unfortunately, no one realised that I was an empath. I could sense energies from people, good and bad, but as a child, I had no way to express it properly. As I became a teenager, all the mood swings got attributed to hormones and I believed this about myself till my late 20s. I thought I was too sensitive, I would ignore my intuition and gut feelings and it cost me a lot of bad decisions and consequences. Only after I had seen my share of losses and disappointments, victories and success, extremely painful health conditions and surgeries, a whirlwind romance and a horrible divorce that I stopped and decided to look within. Something was missing from within me, I decided to live alone, rented a cute little apartment and when I was not working, I spent all my time reading and practising spirituality. I met some amazing people on this journey, who introduced me to various concepts and paths, from Buddhism to Reiki to Law of attraction to Wicca to core Hindu sadhana techniques to meditations of different types. I devoured books mostly on Self-help, Subconscious mind, Psychology, Philosophy, Hinduism, Astrology, Vastu. I even attended church, studied the Bible and sat for Buddhism exams. Slowly I started understanding that I have a gift, a gift of intuition, it is a bit stronger in me than others and I was still figuring out how to utilise this gift. That is when I stumbled onto tarot, I would watch a lot of tarot readings on YouTube, I was highly skeptical and as happens with horoscopes in the newspaper, these readings would be for a collective and would not be specific to me. But something about the art of reading cards attracted me, so I decided to learn it.

"The best way to demystify something is to study it."
- Thorvi Damle

I believe I was led to Tarot. I didn't just wake up one day and know. All the exploration and reading I did along the way, the spiritual practices nudged me into this direction. I trusted my intuition this time and spent a lot of time teaching myself tarot. I practised a lot with the help of my friends and family and attended courses online. Over time, I became confident and adjusted my approach, you see I too started out fortune-telling. I wanted to be all-powerful like a great witch who knew the future, soon I realised that was not the right path. I pursued, and noticed the power of tarot in decision making, as I started doing readings for clients, people I did not know and who were paying for my services.

I also explored other tarot readers, I approached them for my own personal decisions, as I wanted to remove the bias I would have if I did a reading for myself. These readers helped me again to focus on what is more important at that stage in life, though they had more of a fortune-telling approach, still I was able to pick up what I needed and move ahead. It gave me an understanding of how tarot readings are conducted elsewhere.

My focus shifted while interacting with more and more individuals, my clients are all well-educated, high performing and contributing members of the society and I learnt a lot as I started helping them through Tarot. Many times, I would get goose bumps during the reading myself, because remember, I am not advising someone from my own analysis, I only interpret the cards that come out and aid in identifying issues hidden beneath the surface, so the discoveries we would make together in the readings were astonishing and made me respect this art even more. I realised I could do a lot more value add to society by immersing myself in tarot. I took the decision to leave the corporate world and turned to tarot full time. This book is an attempt to bring clarity on tarot, bust myths and provide a background on intuitive decision making.

"My mission is to guide people, ease their internal struggles and help them walk through life empowered, not to make life easy instead make it exciting no matter the circumstances. I want to encourage people to take 100% responsibility for their life and watch miracles unfold once they reset their mindset."
- Thorvi Damle

Remember YOU are the captain of your life; YOU decide your future and Tarot can be Your navigation system.

6

My Interpretation Of Most Misunderstood Tarot Cards

The High Priestess is my signifier card, it represents how I see myself or how I aspire to become one day, both internally and externally. She is seated with a flowing cape, in between two pillars, behind her we see a backdrop with pomegranates, and the scene is set in front of a water body. She wears a crown that has the three phases of the moon (waxing, full and waning) shaped on it and she holds a scroll in her hands. There is a half-moon at her feet and her cape flows over it like water. She wears a cross on her chest and she has a serene expression, almost mysterious like she knows something of grave importance but she will not reveal it so easily. She seems highly intuitive, in touch with the water element and the moon, both symbols of mysticism, occult, spirituality, and hidden information. The moon and water both create scenarios of shadows, play of light and shade, illusions and mystery.

Even on a full moon night, visibility is not great and shadows from trees and objects can cause illusions. Similarly, the depth of water is the greatest illusion, one cannot predict it by looking at the surface. A seemingly clear lake can quickly turn into a life-threatening situation, if we miscalculate the depth. Yet the High Priestess seems to have mastered these illusions, she has the knowledge it seems to create these illusions and more.

When we pull this card in a reading it can have various interpretations depending on the question and the position of this card in a spread. If this is the card of the self, it can mean that the seeker has the qualities of the High Priestess, even if he/she does not realise it, their intuition and knowledge is deep. They should look at empowering their inner voice, their in-built knowledge can lead them out of the situation. There are misleading circumstances and this is not the time to take anything of anyone at face value. The seeker needs to notice any red flags and spend time researching before taking any decision. Above all the seeker should rely on their own instinct, and gut feeling to proceed.

It can also indicate that the seeker should find a mentor or a guide with this energy to lead them through the issue.

The two pillars in the card are black and white and represent duality, and the balance in the middle is the High Priestess herself. She has the ability to maintain balance and take out the concentrated juice if you will of knowledge that can be found in both. The pomegranates in middle eastern culture represent prosperity, fertility, growth and happiness. The flowing nature of her clothes and the water body behind her present, uninhibited flow of energy, the yin or the feminine that does not use brute force, yet is able to flow through the cracks of boulders and over time can convert boulders to dust. The power of intuition, inner knowing, spirituality and flow of energy all encompassed in one.

Photo 2: The High Priestess[10]

---

[10] **Photo Credits:** Cesar Raj photos Pondicherry

Look at the image and write down what emotions or thoughts does this card evoke in you?

Exercise

The Devil Card:

The most infamous card in the deck, one that has led to a lot of misunderstanding and myth. The devil depicts a creature with horns on its head, bearded, fierce-looking with large eyes, the upper body is human and the lower body seems like a beast with claws. He is perched like a bird on top of a block and holds a torch in one hand. The other hand is up in a blessing position. He has wings that resemble a bat and a pentagram on his head. Below him are two people seemingly chained by their necks to the block. A man and a woman, both of them are naked and have horns, they have tails as well. They look calm and not at all as if tied against their will. The man has a tail that seems to be on fire and the woman has a tail that ends in a bunch of grapes.

The image is stark and raw and it does NOT represent the devil in any way. These are the traditional symbols associated with the devil, and the notion of hell. The card itself represents desires and lust, urges and temptations that can bring harm. They also represent lies and deceit, extra-marital affairs and instant gratification. The nature of desires is such that we disassociate ourselves from them if you do something you should not, for example, if you indulge in sexual fantasies and extra-marital affairs, you would not want to believe, you are capable of it yourself, you would want to blame it on someone. Someone made you do it, someone created circumstances that led you to do it, and that someone is this entity created to take on the blame for humanity, the devil. "The devil made me do it" is a famous excuse. We always want to see ourselves in a good light, as perfect as possible, but in reality, we all have flaws and we all have some temptations and desires we cannot always control. This is part of being human and addictions are some of the most common manifestations of such desires. Smoking, drinking, drugs, sex, pornography, junk food, video games etc., are all indicators of desires taking over our mind and we feel we have no control.

When you look closer the chains around their neck are loosely tied, if they choose, they can free themselves, the devil has not kept them captive by force. They have willingly surrendered to him, i.e., they have willingly indulged in destructive behaviour, and are using excuses to avoid responsibility.

This one card can explain a lot about human nature. When the seeker gets this card in a session, it can represent various things. For example, if this appears as an obstacle in a career, it can represent that the seeker needs to remove distractions from life. If the seeker has been spending a lot of time gaming, watching web series, going out partying or is getting distracted by an office affair, they need to identify and rectify this, in order to focus more on their career. The Devil card is a major arcana, in that it does not suggest occasional indulgence, it usually indicates long term addictions or desires that will need more determined effort to overcome. Self-sabotaging patterns and behaviours that have been practised subconsciously over years.

In a relationship reading, it can also indicate toxic relationships, domestic violence and emotional manipulation. As I mentioned earlier, it depends on the question and the other cards in the spread, it can also indicate thought patterns that are toxic and serve no purpose. Although it sounds ominous and scary, I want to bring into focus the fact that the two individuals on the card are here voluntarily, no one is forcing them to do anything against their will, and hence they hold the power to move away and break free from these chains. It is a matter of deciding and sticking to the decisions, the seeker holds the power in any situation to change the course of life.

Photo 3: The Devil[11]

---

[11] **Photo Credits:** Cesar Raj photos Pondicherry

Question to ask yourself, what are you addicted to, that is not serving any higher purpose? Are you indulging in any behaviour or pattern, that may be self-sabotaging?

Exercise

The Tower Card:

The card shows a dark night, lightning striking a tall tower and destroying the top part of the tower. This top part is shaped like the crown and the tower is on fire. Two people are shown falling out of the burning tower as smoke rushes out of it. They seem to be screaming out of the sheer shock of the incident. An unexpected turn of events that have endangered their life. They seem to be part of the royalty, based on the clothes they are wearing and the fact that they live in a tower, the crown falling on the side is an indication too. This tower is steeped high on top of a hill and what seems like the hill made of ice way above in the clouds.

This card often evokes fear and uncertainty. It usually indicates a sudden turn of events, unexpected happenings, pivotal turning points that catch one off-guard.

It also represents the humbling of the ego, if one has been too proud and vain of success, something will happen that will shake this pride and make the seeker question his/her purpose. Depending on the question and the card spread, this card can indicate loss of some kind or revealing of some information that will bring a drastic change. It indicates information that will appear suddenly but shake your belief either in someone or some circumstance. And unfortunately, this will be painful, it has a shock element to it.

It can indicate loss of job, or finances, unexpected misunderstandings within relationships, health issues, movement from a place, or to give a recent example, the way the pandemic hit the tourism and food industry, nothing could prepare the world for this pandemic. Now, this may seem like classic doomsday fortune-telling, but it is in fact, the opposite. The tower moment in life is unexpected, hence we cannot predict how it will exactly pan out. The purpose of this card is to warn the seeker, if he/she has been slacking in any area, or taking things for granted in any relationship a tower moment can be expected to shift the course of life. I liken the tower card to how astrology views eclipses. Eclipses are not rare, they occur at least four times a year, yet these are powerful portals of energy shifts. They are described as the course correctors of one's life. For example, Frank has been working in the US for the past 10 years, and he has become stagnant in his career. He knows that for his domain, better job prospects are available in Canada, yet he has become so comfortable with this daily life in the US that he has been procrastinating on the change. He is literally sitting on the decision and postponing it because subconsciously he does not want to deal with the mess of moving to another country, even if it means dying a slow internal death in his current job. He is miserable working there; he is not intellectually being challenged and his innovative brain has gone to sleep long ago. An eclipse, which occurs in a particular part of his horoscope, can trigger a tower moment, where his company fires him for no solid reason. Now, he is forced to look at moving to another country and finding a job more suited for his life's journey. He may get upset, curse his luck, whine and complain for a few months, but maybe after a year when he looks back at the moment he was laid off, he would be grateful it happened, because he is now at a much happier place in life, with a fulfilling job, better pay and better work-life balance.

I always look at the tower card as a course corrector. It comes to warn us to brace ourselves for impact, it may not make any sense at that moment but when you look back at life, it will fall in place perfectly. It makes us upset and extremely uncomfortable at times, but remember that it will appear for a higher good over time.

Photo 4: The Tower[12]

Do you remember any such tower moments in your life? Something so drastic, you never imagined it, and it caused you heartache but later fell in place in life?

---

[12] **Photo Credits:** Cesar Raj photos Pondicherry

Exercise

The Death Card:

One of the famous cards used in media, television, and movies to create a sensation. This is one of the cards that can cause a lot of strife, if not interpreted the right way. The card shows a skeletal figure in a knight's armour on a white horse. He holds a black flag with a white rose on it. He is almost walking over the dead laying on the ground and a bishop in golden robes is standing in front of him holding his hands together in prayer. A young child is standing beside him, but he is not afraid of the figure on the horse. There appears to be a woman kneeling beside him, looking away as if in grief. In the background, you can see a river and beyond it, the sun is rising in all its glory between two towers.

Let me make it very clear, No one can predict death. Even if a highly intuitive person has the ability to predict death, this is not something one must aspire to know. Spiritually inclined individuals will never predict someone's death and personally, I do not take cards for this. There have been clients in the past who wanted to know when they will die. Curiosity about birth and death is natural, but knowing one's death may not make life any easier. Now that this is clear, The Death card represents transformation, not physical death. It represents the transformation that demands sacrifice and patience. Transformation in itself is the death of the old version, and the birth of the new version. Like the phoenix bird, that is said to shed all its feathers and then become ash and from this ash, it arises again as a young newborn phoenix. Similarly, this card indicates some uncomfortable situations that will force you to evolve, force you to take decisions you have been avoiding to take, force you to move towards new opportunities. This also indicates the death of a relationship, if the seeker has been holding onto a relationship that has long ago died, this could indicate that it is time to move on.

We usually associate comfort with progress, but that is so not true. Comfort is great for a short while, but it leads to stagnancy in life. It is different from being satisfied and content, so we need to understand the difference. Stagnancy is when you feel you are stuck in a routine that does not motivate you, yet you choose to stay because things are comfortable externally. You are scared to rock the boat and history is proof that those who chose comfort did not achieve anything great in life. When this card is drawn, depending on the question, either you have been through a painful transformation or it is a sign that there is going to be a transformation and one must be prepared mentally for it. Though it sounds scary, knowledge of this information can help us tremendously in facing life situations, we are aware and hence do not react to a situation instead we respond to it.

"Tarot gives you the ability to respond to a situation rather than react to it, and that is real personal power."
- Thorvi Damle

Look at the expression of the bishop/priest, he is worshipping this figure not out of fear but out of understanding. This card also indicates spiritual awakening and spiritual transformation and most of the time this comes through painful situations. But looking at the bigger picture is what will help you pass through this victoriously. The woman on her knees is refusing to look at the figure, she is looking away and hence she sees only the suffering in this situation. The child on the other hand is looking at the figure in awe and wonderment, not afraid but curious. Which one will you choose to be? That is the question one needs to ask oneself.

Photo 5: The Death[13]

Have you felt this death energy in life? If yes, what did you do to overcome it?

---

[13] **Photo Credits:** Cesar Raj photos Pondicherry

Exercise

The Sun card:

I want to share one more card, this time the happiest card in the tarot deck. Tarot is not always about painful growth, it has many cards, which provide hope, happiness, new beginnings, love, joy and more. The Sun card is the happiest card of the tarot deck, and it embodies all the goodness of the Sun.

Photo 6: The Sun[14]

---

[14] **Photo Credits:** Cesar Raj photos Pondicherry

The card shows a naked baby, or a cherub baby, with a wreath of sunflowers on its head, riding a white horse and holding an orange flag. The Sun is shining in all its glory in the background which flaunts a sunflower field. The card is pure sunshine after what feels like an eternity of darkness. It represents success, being in the limelight, rewards, recognition, fame, etc. If it is accompanied by The Empress card, it can also indicate pregnancy, fertility and childbirth. It indicates a time of basking in glory and enjoying the rewards of hard work or good karma paying off. Like the Sun shines a light on the entire world as soon as it rises every morning, the Sun card overpowers the entire reading again depending on its position in the card spread. It also represents ego, pride or too much focus on the self. But most of the time, it indicates pure happiness without any hidden aspects. Happiness that feels real and is not anything you will pay for later.

The ultimate state of mind we all aspire for is the Sun card. A state where we are at our best physically, emotionally, financially, when we are adored and liked by those around us, when we are recognized for our talents and contribution to the world, where we have no insecurities and are sure of our own strengths and weaknesses. A state of ultimate personal power and a bit of external power as well, where we walk through our life like the emperor, when things just fall in place organically and one need not lift a finger. It is a welcome card in any reading and though it may not be an immediate manifestation any indication of this state is more than joyous. We are all born to be the sun in our lives, shine bright the light we have within, the uniqueness we bring into this world just by existing. This card brings hope if you have been working hard but nothing has been manifesting externally.

Remember the sun moments of your life, when did you feel on top of the world? When was the last time you were appreciated or rewarded either at work or by family and close ones? When were you last celebrated?

Exercise

7

Psychology of Tarot & Carl Jung

"Real power lies in understanding the underlying causes of feelings and emotions that drive any decision."
- Thorvi Damle

Sreesha was a 28-year-old IT worker, he was doing fairly well in his career but it felt a bit stagnant. He was working hard and though his manager identified him as a key team member, it did not reflect in growth. The work had also started getting monotonous and he felt he was doing the same thing again and again; he had gotten really good at it and the tasks would get completed but he was not doing anything different. He felt he was stuck, he looked at gathering information from colleagues and friends, he read articles on LinkedIn and he made up a list of courses he could do to get ahead in his career. He had identified a few which would cost him his savings and required a significant amount of time and effort. In his personal life, he had been dating a girl for many years now and things seemed to be going good. He was comfortable in the relationship, but he didn't want to marry so soon. They both had discussed this on several occasions, and he had assumed she was on board. Suddenly one day, she called him and asked him to decide. Her parents were forcing her to get married and she agreed with them, she wanted to settle down and if he was not up for it, she suggested ending the relationship. He was shocked, he had not expected it and this woke him up to reality. Meanwhile, he was getting increasingly frustrated at work and had started arguing with team members and feeling like no one recognized his contributions. He wanted to grow and he wanted it fast, he wanted the next designation and salary hike that he knew he was worthy of, but suddenly he could not wait any longer. With so much weighing on him, he started finding ways to cope with it and one weekend drank a bit too much with his friends, he ended up creating a huge scene, his friends had to take him home and ensure he was alright. The next day, he woke up with a splitting headache, stumbled out of bed and managed to open his eyes. His best friend of 20 plus years was standing there, holding a cup of strong coffee, but without the usual smile on his face. Sreesha knew he had crossed a limit last night and this was not at all his usual self, he knew a lecture was en route from his best friend. Instead, his friend waited for him to finish the coffee and freshen up, he took him out for a scrumptious brunch and handed him the number of a friend. He asked Sreesha to call up and book a tarot session. Sreesha just laughed at him and said he does not need voodoo and magic, but his friend pressed on and he finally gave in.

Reluctantly, he made the call and booked the session. It was a voice call session and the person on the other side sounded normal, there was no voodoo talk. She asked him to find a quiet space, take a few deep breaths and talk to her about the most pressing questions on his mind. He was skeptical, and hence he decided to ask about his career first. Should he go for that expensive course to enhance his chances? Will he get promoted or get a salary hike? As the tarot practitioner was shuffling his cards and laying them out, she mentioned something that blew his mind. She did not know him and did not know his friend so well, she just relayed what the cards told her. She said there is something deeper that is affecting his sudden restlessness and his career is only the surface, she said there is a romantic element that is triggering his emotions. They further discussed and pulled cards on the relationship and suddenly, it was getting clearer to Sreesha. The decision of his girlfriend had triggered insecurities within him, he had been shaken up and suddenly found himself in a situation he could not control. The emotions within spilt over into his career and instead of being patient and working towards his goals, he could not slow down anymore, he dreamt of shortcuts to growing and though he knew deep within, this course would not help much, he wanted something, something big to commit to and distract himself, so he could avoid having to deal with the real issue at hand. He asked the tarot practitioner to pull cards on his relationship and he got clarity, to respect the other person's decision but not lose his individuality. No one should be pushing him around to do something he is not ready to do, though he loved this girl, he needed to have an honest conversation with himself on what he could and could not provide in this relationship and he suddenly, felt a new found confidence that though the decisions he would take were difficult, it was not the end of the world. He spent the next few days grounding himself; he took a few days off and travelled solo to a nearby place and kept his cell phone away. He thought about the points they had discussed and noted down what he really felt and wanted from life.

After he hung up the phone, he was different, did all his problems go away? No, but he had enough clarity to make decisions that gave him the best possible outcomes and isn't that what we all need. What did tarot do here? Tarot did not predict whether he will marry that girl or whether he will get a promotion after that course, tarot simply showed the mirror where the root cause lay. You may be wondering, he did not even pick the cards himself, this was a voice call, how is this possible? I know, it is possible because that is how I do 95% of my readings, over voice calls. Let me explain. If you have watched the movie Avatar, there is a scene where the blue aliens connect themselves to the tree of knowledge, all of them are connected to the universal consciousness, similarly, a tarot practitioner can connect with someone's energies even remotely by developing the skill of meditation and intuition. They become the medium and can channel someone else's intuition through the cards, and even during meditation.

The story gives a glimpse of one scenario in which tarot helped him make intuitive decisions, helped him look at the root cause of his restlessness and helped him gain courage and faith in his own decision making. Though it seems little, in my experience it is a lot. Unfortunately, this is a huge gap in most people's decision-making skills. Once they cross it they feel much better, they have a lot of confidence, they can articulate their feelings better and not just in the area of life they had questions on, all areas of life suddenly seem to change. A disclaimer, not all tarot readers have this approach, nearly 90% still focus only on fortune-telling. I have nothing against fortune-telling, and I find it fascinating. During my own sessions, I do get inputs of predictions and they have come true, but I see the potential of tarot to be much more effective in empowering people.

Psychology of Tarot:

To understand a bit more of how tarot cards and the images and symbols evoke certain mental states and how these can be universally interpreted in the same way, we can look to Carl Gustav Jung. He was a famous psychiatrist and psychotherapist, who worked extensively on explaining what he called universal archetypes. For example, the picture of a mother and child will invoke similar emotions and responses from humans across the world, that of motherhood, love, nurturing etc. How are all humans responding to an image in a similar fashion? Jung explained three layers of the human psyche[15], the ego, the personal unconscious and the collective unconscious.

The ego represents the conscious mind as it comprises the thoughts, memories, and emotions a person is aware of. The ego is largely responsible for feelings of identity and continuity.

The personal unconscious is essentially the same as Freud's version of the unconscious. The personal unconscious contains temporarily forgotten information and repressed memories.

The collective unconscious is a universal version of the personal unconscious, holding mental patterns, or memory traces, which are shared with other members of the human species (Jung, 1928). These ancestral memories, which Jung called archetypes, are represented by universal themes in various cultures, as expressed through literature, art, and dreams.

This collective unconscious which I like to refer to, as universal consciousness, is the invisible net that encompasses us all. This is the compassionate

---

[15] www.simplypsychology.org/carl-jung.html

energy of mother nature that has tied us all together as one human race, not separate from nature but being nature itself. It is really fascinating that humans across the world, irrespective of religion, status, nationality, be it a successful lawyer in New York or a member of the aboriginal tribe in the forest, all smile when we are happy and cry when we are sad, we all raise arms or fold arms and look up to the sky when we think of God, every religion teaches love, respect and the power of faith. How can that be?

Art is another powerful and beautiful way to connect with others, visit art museums as much as possible, you will start noticing the symbols, patterns, colours and emotions that each art piece evokes, and many of them relay the message without the need for an explanation. Similarly, tarot cards evoke the messages from the universal consciousness as well as the seeker's energy to arrive at analysis of the issue at hand. In the earlier chapter, you would have felt this connection as you explored some of the cards and wrote down your experiences with the concept and what the images evoked in you.

Another popular theory is Jung's Theory of Synchronicity. Around 1930, he explained the Jungian Theory of Synchronicity, when two or more events seem to be related but cannot be adequately explained by cause and effect, the theory of how and why the events occur together is synchronicity. According to Jung, synchronicity explained the attuning of a psychic state with external events.

I would like to share an incident from my life that will help you understand this better. This happened to me and my close friend Ramya (a practising psychiatrist in New Zealand), in 2018. I was visiting her in New Zealand, for a few weeks and during that stay she had to attend a conference in Australia for 3-4 days. I stayed back in New Zealand. I was wandering the local mall in Hamilton and stumbled upon a stationery store named Typo. Being a lover of stationery items, especially notebooks, diaries and pens, I stepped in and like a child at the candy store, I spent over an hour, wide-eyed and excited about everything in that store. The store was stocked with new year stock of calendars, planners, diaries and other fancy items. Finally, I picked up a few things, one of them was a sparkly pink notebook and it was the favourite of my shopping haul that day. The next few days, I spent sightseeing and since Ramya was busy at the conference we barely spoke; I did not find time to mention the shopping to her. She returned in a few days and we went to pick her up. She got into the car and handed me a packet; it was a surprise gift. It was neatly wrapped in brown paper and I was super excited to open it. I had no clue what was inside. As I ripped away the wrapping paper, I found a sparkly pink notebook with my name etched on it. I could not believe my eyes; it was the exact kind of notebook I had picked up a few days ago. When we exchanged details of our days, we figured that around the same time that I was shopping in a Typo store in New Zealand, she happened to walk into the Typo store in Australia and picked up the same notebook as a gift for me. We had never discussed notebooks before, this was not something I planned to buy or aspired to own. This was synchronicity, two events that happened independent of each other, yet seem to be profoundly interconnected. It was a goosebump moment for us, we knew being close friends we are connected on a higher plane and have had other telepathic experiences but this was mind-blowing and coincidence is not enough term to explain it away. I still have the two notebooks, and every time I look at them, I am reminded of the power of the inner guidance system, of universal consciousness and the power that we do not see. It is a knowing, deeper than a mindless coincidence, one of the examples of Jung's theory of synchronicity.

The picking and choosing of tarot cards are similar, I experience it in all tarot readings I have done so far, the cards pulled will perfectly align with the issue at hand. It does not take away from the importance of tarot's role as an advisor and guide, I believe it instead strengthens its position.

Jung also dabbled in tools of decision making, he practised the art of I Ching, a Chinese divination tool that uses hexagrams to derive answers and is recorded way back in history as far as 475-221 BC China. Jung wrote in the foreword to the book on I Ching translated to German by, Richard Wilhelm

"For more than thirty years I have interested myself in this oracle technique, or method of exploring the unconscious, for it has seemed to me of uncommon significance. I was already fairly familiar with, the I Ching when I first met Wilhelm in the early nineteen twenties; he confirmed for me then what I already knew, and taught me many things more"

Jung is said to have used I Ching with patients in psychotherapy to derive more information and understand deeper meanings to their issues[16].

We are not always able to express everything we feel, we experience or even what we dream and tools like I Ching and tarot can help us express these even to ourselves. My approach to tarot is not purely based on psychology, I am not a certified psychoanalyst or a medical professional, and hence I only take inspiration from these works. There is increasing curiosity and experiments by psychotherapists with tarot, using tarot and the concept of archetypes by Jung, these therapists are trying to get a deeper understanding of the human mind. As they explore more, tarot will be a central guiding tool for future generations. We can save a lot of heartache and confusion as we understand ourselves better with each tarot session and realise the power that lies within us to elevate our lives.

"Tarot is above all a symbolic system of self-knowledge, self-integration, and self-transformation. Vital to integration is the union of opposites within, a process which Jung says 'on a higher

---

[16] www.carl-jung.net/iching.html

level of consciousness is not a rational thing, nor is it a matter of will; it is a psychic process of development which expresses itself in symbols" - Richard Roberts, The original Tarot & You

Role of Faith & Patience in success:

Over the years, I have seen two major themes pop up as learnings from the majority of the tarot sessions, two lessons that we all know but very few apply in life. The two main teachings of all religions and spiritual practices and famously associated with Shirdi Sai Baba, Shraddha and Saburi i.e., Faith and Patience. They are not new and are seldom fast-moving traits, and hence not always appealing. Their power is often underrated and yet those who have invested in them have reaped big awards.

There was a famous experiment conducted in the 1960s-70s by psychologist Walter Mischel to study self-control in young children and the prolonged effects of this as they grow into adults. The researchers placed a bowl with a marshmallow (sweet treat) on a table in an empty room, children from age groups 3 to 5 years were tested individually. They are told that they should wait in the room while the researchers left, if they did not eat the marshmallow on the table till the researchers returned, they would be rewarded with two marshmallows, if they ate this, they would not get another treat. Some children controlled themselves and waited for the researchers to return, enjoying the reward of two treats. Some children could not control themselves and were willing to sacrifice the reward for immediate satisfaction. Remember, the children were left alone in the room and hence it was purely their decision. The researchers then followed these children through the years of their growth. Children who demonstrated self-control during the marshmallow test were more successful in life, had better scores, landed high paying jobs, excelled at sports and other activities, were better in maintaining relationships compared to the children who did not demonstrate self-control, who were found to be lacking in all the above fields in life, they made rash decisions, got involved in drugs and in general had a poorer outcome.

Which category do you fall in? Can you sacrifice instant gratification for a long-term goal? I probably fall into the latter category, judging from the number of times I have attempted to give up sugar and failed in a few days. Be extremely honest with yourself, this will help you understand and correct your patterns sooner. Observe the people around you whom you deem successful, do you see these traits in them? An athlete competing for the Olympics needs to train every single day for four years, for one day of glory. He/she needs to maintain the levels of excitement, enthusiasm for prolonged periods of time. As humans, they are bound to have good days and bad days, a lot can happen in the span of 4 years. What keeps them going is faith and patience, faith that they will win and patience to train every single day. If you find yourself complaining a lot about something in life, ask yourself what you are doing about it, are you taking action? Do you have faith that things will change? Are you practising patience and showing up every day trying to find a solution? If the answer is No, then you have no right to complain, if the answer is Yes, then continue showing up and continue working towards a change, but stop complaining as complaining will increase the time gap between you and the solution. Place your bets on faith and patience and miracles will happen. You will only be able to do this with awareness of your own thoughts and patterns. Tarot can bring you that in an instant. You can ask the tarot practitioner to pull cards on your current thinking patterns, what is helping you and what needs to be changed. A simple three-card spread that can give you a treasure of knowledge in return.

"Awareness is the Elixir of Life."
- Thorvi Damle

8

A Brief History Of Tarot

Would you like to time travel given the chance? I am taking you now on a short trip in my time machine, come on, hop into the time machine and fasten your seatbelt. Are you ready? Pushing the button 5,4,3,2,1 and blasting off to the 1700s.

We are now in France in the late 1700s, peeking through a window of a rich aristocrat's house. It is a cold winter afternoon and as we peek in through this window, we see a luxurious parlour adorned with velvet curtains ending with tassels, silk upholstery, golden candle holders, gold-rimmed chairs with velvet cushions. The walls look majestic with huge portraits of nobility and the floors covered with exquisitely woven carpets. There is a huge fireplace with a burning blaze keeping this room warm and cosy, the mantle pieces above look like antiques brought in from distant traders. A daunting crystal chandelier hangs on the ceiling representing the epitome of luxury and privilege of the aristocrats, who are alas threatened as the French revolution is at its peak and their lot is being persecuted. There are lords and ladies surrounding a huge wooden table, leaning over to listen intently to a fortune teller. She has a grim expression on her face, as she lays out the cards in front of her and shakes her head. The atmosphere is tense with anticipation, all of them are looking at her with bated breaths. She is the most famous cartomancer (one who practises cartomancy) and fortune teller in Europe, Madame Lenormand[17] and she has predicted a lot during these uncertain times of the revolution that have come to pass. She is also the trusted council of the Queen herself, Queen Josephine, Napoleon Bonaparte's wife. Even the Tsar of Russia Alexander would invite her for counsel later in 1814. What she predicts is a grim future for some of them, and narrow escapes for the lucky few.

Oh, shoot! We need to get back now, the fuel metre on the time machine is beeping, we will continue the story back into the future. Hop on and blast off again to 2022.

Continuing our history session, Josephine had immense trust in her cartomancer and fortune

---

[17] The Essential Lenormand: Your Guide to Precise 7 Practical Fortunetelling by Rana George

teller Madame Lenormand. Josephine was married earlier to Alexandre, Vicomte de Beauharnais and had been arrested along with him in 1794, charged as enemies of the French revolution. In jail, she met Madame Lenormand who had also been arrested on similar charges. Josephine was in an unhappy marriage with two children and now was in jail. She desperately needed to know her future, to get some assurance of hope, would she die in the jail, and even if she was released, would she go back to the miserable life with her husband. She heard from inmates that there was a fortune teller in the same jail. She sent a message to her, this was her last hope. Madame Lenormand responded to her letter, she predicted that Alexandre will be killed and Josephine will be released. She went on to predict that Josephine will have great fortune in her life. As predicted, Josephine's husband was executed and she was let free shortly after.

Later in life, she married Napoleon Bonaparte and became the Queen of France. Madame Lenormand is said to have helped her in the decision to marry Napoleon, and had predicted he would become the king. Though Napoleon himself did not believe in the occult, he thought it was all hearsay and a waste of time. His wife on the other hand believed and advocated it throughout her life, catapulting Madame Lenormand as one of the most celebrated and sought-after fortune tellers in history who made cartomancy popular. Madame Lenormand may not have used the exact set of cards that we see now in modern tarot, but her contribution to increasing its popularity cannot be denied.

The tarot as we know it has been around since the 15th century said to have been created in Italy. They say the term tarot comes from Tarocchi (an Italian game before Tarot). These were hand-painted cards commissioned by the Duke of Milan, Francesco Visconti as early as 1415 and are also known as the Visconti-Sforza tarots.

But cards similar to tarot used for divination and fortune-telling have been found from well before this time as well. It is believed that hand-painted cards were used in China as a card game and slowly spread to Islamic countries and reached Europe. The gypsies used these cards for fortune-telling and most of the history is not written as the Church banned tarot readings and people were hunted for practising any form of divination, they termed it witchcraft. People still practised tarot, but it was hidden to avoid persecution. I would like to salute the bravery of people from these times, to continue practising something under the constant threat of death and yet passing it on from one generation to another, their dedication kept this alive. It is unfortunate that even now certain countries look at tarot as evil, the Arab nations forbid any kind of fortune-telling and in certain countries it is illegal. Let us hope that with more awareness we can convince people to see the uses of this tool, knowledge will also safeguard from con artists who swindle money in the name of tarot.

Coming back to the tarot decks, the Rider-Waite-Smith deck is the most popular basic tarot deck used widely today and it revolutionised tarot and made it available to the masses. Arthur Edward Waite, a renowned occultist of the modern era, commissioned Pamela Colman Smith, an artist to create the deck and it was published by William Rider & Son in London in 1909. This deck forms the basis for all modern tarot decks available. They published the deck with a guide book and included the meanings to enable anyone to learn and try out this tool. Tarot like many other divination tools has been around for a long time and has survived for so long because it has helped countless individuals navigate difficult life situations.

A simple explanation of what the heck is Tarot:

Tarot is part of Cartomancy, the art of divination using cards. Tarot (pronounced with last T silent) is a set of 78 cards used in divination. They are similar to regular playing cards, they have 56 cards named Minor Arcana. These are split into four categories and contain cards from Ace till Ten in each category (Wands, Swords, Cups & Pentacles) and then instead of three court cards (Jack, Queen, King) they have four court cards (Page, Knight, Queen and King), the rest of the 22 cards are unique to Tarot and are known as the Major Arcana.

Minor Arcana represent minor or moving life events, which have short term effects on our lives. Major Arcana, as the name suggests, represents major life lessons, major events that have more effect on our lives.

This book is not going to turn you into a tarot reader, or a witch or a wizard. This is just basic information to make you a little world-wise. Fear has stemmed due to misinformation, and also the fact that religious institutions a few hundred years ago persecuted free thinkers under the name of witchcraft. Thousands were burnt at the stakes of being accused of occult practices or of being witches, these years of persecution forced intuitive tarot readers to continue this art in hiding.

These cards are used as a medium or a tool to interpret messages from the subconscious as well as higher powers. The cards contain images and numbers and although each card has a basic meaning attached to it, it depends on the tarot practitioner how these are interpreted. They may change depending on the question and seeker. For example, The Death card does not indicate death, it indicates transformation because transformation is the death of the old self, and the birth of the new self.

Congratulations, you now know more about this unique art than most people and can take an informed decision on including tarot in your decision-making process. But wait, there is a bit more waiting for you in the next chapter that will help you tie this all up into a neat, practical bundle.

Conclusion

Four Steps To Elevate Method

If you have been living life without a strategy, it is high time you work on one. The strategy may sound like a business term but it is just deliberate living, creating a life that gives you maximum chances of survival, of happiness, of peace and of excellence. Who would not want that?

Introducing the "Four steps to elevate" method that will catapult you into another level of being human. If you implement this, people around you will want to know your secret to success. Subtle, slow yet steady changes will occur first within you and then in your external circumstances but for people looking from the outside, it will be nothing short of overnight change.

The two horses on your success chariot will need to be Faith and Patience, an unwavering belief in yourself and the ability to put in the work. Tarot will be the navigation system, making you aware of the speed bumps, potholes, shortest routes and oasis en route.

FOUR-STEP METHOD:

1. Reduce decision fatigue
2. Recruit your pit crew
3. Take Action
4. Evolve

1. Reducing stress must be your first line of defence. We are all dealing with a lot of stress, and hence firefighting throughout the day has started to seem normal. It is not normal; you were not born to put our fires throughout the day. Remember, Decision fatigue is real, it cannot be fixed overnight and it cannot be ignored for long. The stress from decision fatigue is already trickling into major life decisions and interfering with the quality of your life and those dependent on you. Explore the thousands of free apps, videos and meditative practices. Keep it fun, try a walking meditation or put reminders on your phone to take one minute out every two hours to just observe your breathing. Get up from your seat and walk around, have a glass of water, start small and build your way up to find the perfect

fit for you when it comes to mindfulness. You will be amazed at the results in just a few days. It is taking back a few minutes in a day for your mental health, an investment that will never let you down, it will not crash like the stock market, the mindfulness market is always bullish. Get good at delegating work, you are not superman/woman. I remember an interview of Indira Nooyi, former Chairperson & CEO of PepsiCo, she mentioned that while she was working as a CEO, she was also a mother of two daughters. Her daughter would call her office during the day asking permission to play videogames and she had given a set of questions to her assistant to ask her daughter on these calls, like "Did you complete your homework?" and her assistant would answer, and help with these calls with her daughters. Later, the assistant would catch her up on when and why her daughter called in. Please don't start judging her parenting skills here, the point is accepting that you are not God, you cannot be there all the time for everyone. You need to delegate whatever possible and whenever possible to help remove your decision fatigue. What she did here was just that, she put in mechanisms to help her reduce her decision fatigue. So, get clever, get innovative and remember you are doing yourself the favour, by reducing decision fatigue, you become more capable as a person to support your family & colleagues in times of actual need. Recruit family members, friends, colleagues even bosses, yes ask for help, delegate and create mechanisms so that you can give your 100%.

2. We all need allies to grow, even the strongest of dictators need a team of trusted people around them. If you watch Formula One racing, you will notice that the cars need to take short breaks to fuel up, change tires, do maintenance checks etc. before they zoom into the race again. The team of mechanics who work on the racing car is known as the pit crew. They do all of these maintenance checks and changes within 12 seconds, efficiently and focused on one thing, helping the driver win the race. Create your own pit crew, people who truly are invested in you and will jump in for those 12-second pit stops in life. You will be surprised that your pit crew rarely includes a family member, very rarely. I recommend recruiting friends and professionals. My pit crew includes my close friends, my therapist, my physiotherapist, my spiritual guides, and professional mentors. These are the people

who will help me review, detect and course correct. Unlike the recruits we saw earlier to delegate daily tasks, your pit crew will be an inner circle. Focused on the bigger picture, on your goals, ambitions, your mental health and rooting for your success as an individual. A tarot practitioner is a **must** in your pit crew, he/she is a combination of a therapist, spiritual guide, philosopher and mentor. The tarot practitioner does NOT replace these individuals, he/she holds a mirror for your inner self to observe, review and in turn helps the rest of the pit crew to efficiently guide you. You need to test and try and find the right tarot practitioner for you, who will work with you to unearth hidden patterns and messages. With the knowledge and awareness of yourself and the circumstances, you can develop your next steps and strategies to thrive.

PIT CREW
Review-----Detect-----Course Correct

3. 6th Grade physics teaches us the definition of Work Done "Work is done when a force acts upon an object to cause a displacement". The key to note is work is only done when displacement occurs, if the object does not move, no matter how much force is applied,

work is not considered to be done. Wishful thinking is like force being applied without displacement. Action is required to bring dreams into reality, action along with dreams lead to manifestation. Your pit crew can only help you in the maintenance of the car for short bursts of time, you need to drive the car, you need to practise the skills and compete with other drivers. A tarot practitioner will guide you and also advise on what needs to be worked on, what needs to be changed and if you follow through you will be amazed by the results. Take charge of your life, if the tarot practitioner advises you to hold your tongue for the next few months and avoid just stating your mind, take the effort to actually stop before you speak, measure your words and speak only what is necessary. You will be amazed at the power of silence, influencing people without words. Alternatively, he/she may advise you to speak up, to share your thoughts, to be brave and put forth your ideas in a team meeting, then just do it, no matter how scary it may be, just jump in with faith and see the doors that it can unlock for you. If you expect results without any effort, it is foolishness, even Cinderella had to physically go to the ball to find her prince charming.

4. Evolution is the driving force behind everything we do. The constant need to improve the chances of survival is what nature strives to do, every species of life works on this principle. We evolved physically to the two-legged creatures as per the natural demand of evolution, but from here onwards evolution is no longer physical. We have created such comfortable environments thanks to technology, we no longer need to evolve physically. The need then is shifted to the mental and spiritual plane. Evolution is now a mind game, and unless you evolve you cannot survive. You may survive physically but your genetics will not in the long run. The Evolution of the mind, of the inner self, needs awareness that is the starting point. Steps, 1 through 3 help you bring in awareness, help you start taking action as well, but life happens in waves, it is not static. And when unknown factors hit us, like the pandemic in 2020, those who survived observed, adjusted their approach and found workarounds to become successful despite the pandemic. Those who did not are still crying and complaining about how unfair life is. My strong advice is to stay away from people who always complain, they will never grow and will never let you grow. These people love being victims and

always point the finger outwards for their failures. Many businesses changed their working model, started home delivery of products and cataloguing products on social media for better reach. Traditionally, businesses that never needed technology, jumped onto the social media waggon to find ways to keep the business going. Apply the same to yourself, challenges will come and we cannot always predict them, but observing, course correcting and adapting will take you places. Be flexible in your approach towards life, remember, change is the only constant.

Tarot is your shortcut to success; it is the transporter key that can open up portals for you. You need not learn it or understand it to use it. Bypass your stress, gain valuable time otherwise wasted on deliberation and confusion, build confidence in your own decision-making skills. Half the battle is won with confidence and when it is you creating your own life strategy, Tarot can provide the invaluable validation to step ahead confidently.

"Clarity makes the difference between unconscious and deliberate living."
– Thorvi Damle

The End

Review Ask

Love this book? Don't forget to
leave a review!
thorvimdamle@gmail.com

Every review matters, and it matters a *lot!*
Thank you in advance!

Explore More from Thorvi!

Want to experience Tarot with Thorvi? Visit her website to book your session today https://www.Thorvidamle.com/

While there, check out her blog for life lessons, inspirations, and relatable posts that will force you to look at things in a different way

If you prefer to listen, check out her podcast show "Soulfully Thorvi" available on Spotify, Apple podcasts, Google podcasts, Audible and all other major audio streaming apps.

https://soulfullythorvi.buzzsprout.com/

Author Bio

Thorvi Damle

Thorvi was born in Pune and grew up in the beautiful town of Pondicherry, with French colonial and local Tamil influences. She began her career in the corporate world, working in a prestigious organisation where she led several global projects. Parallel to this, her interest in spirituality, intuition, philosophy and psychology meant she devoured books and learnt from mentors & guides.

Tarot became her medium of choice and ever since she has guided countless individuals through difficult life situations. Guided by cosmic events, she turned her passions into her profession and is now a sought-after tarot practitioner, writer and podcast host. She has developed a unique approach to the psychic art of tarot, one that combines the power of intuition with the approach of project management, *shifting focus from predictions to solutions*. Her mission is to ease people's internal struggles and help them walk through life empowered, not to make life easy instead make it exciting no matter the circumstances.

Thorvi loves delving into the unknown and finding solutions that are otherwise hidden. When she is not writing or pulling out tarot cards, you will find her reading a book, spending time with animals, cooking or travelling.

Her brand is **Thorvi,** *an intuitive guidance* company providing tarot sessions and guidance solutions.

At her website www.thorvidamle.com you can book a personal tarot session with her. You can also read her blog and listen to her podcast where she shares unique perspectives on life's challenges, discussing a range of topics from mythology to psychology.

CPSIA information can be obtained
at www.ICGtesting.com
Printed in the USA
BVHW071017200922
647501BV00001B/101